High Scorer's Choice Series

IELTS 5 Practice Tests

General Set 3

(Tests No. 11-15)

High Scorer's Choice Series, Book 6
IELTS 5 Practice Tests, General Set 3 (Tests No. 11–15)
ISBN 9780648000037
Copyright © 2017 Simone Braverman, Robert Nicholson.
First Edition May 2017
Updated February 2023

Available in print and digital formats
Accompanying audio recordings to be downloaded on the following webpage:
https://www.ielts-blog.com/ielts-practice-tests-downloads/

IELTS® is a registered trademark of University of Cambridge ESOL, the British Council, and IDP Education Australia, which neither sponsor nor endorse this book.

To contact the authors:
Email: simone@ielts-blog.com
Website: www.ielts-blog.com

Acknowledgements

The authors hereby acknowledge the following websites for their contributions to this book (see the webpage below for a complete list):

www.ielts-blog.com/acknowledgements/

While every effort has been made to contact copyright holders it has not been possible to identify all sources of the material used. The authors and publisher would in such instances welcome information from copyright holders to rectify any errors or omissions

Praise for
High Scorer's Choice Practice Tests

"I am a teacher from Australia. I had a Chinese friend who is studying for the exam and I used these [tests] to help him. I think the papers are very professional and useful. Many of the commercial practice papers are not culturally sensitive but this was not a problem with your tests."
- *Margaretta from Australia*

"I found out that your practice papers are excellent. I took my IELTS on March 11th and got an Overall Band 8 with listening – 8, reading – 9, writing – 7 and speaking – 7. I spent one month on preparation."
- *Dr Yadana from London, UK*

"I must tell you that the sample tests I have purchased from you have been the key to my preparation for the IELTS. Being employed full time I do not have the time to attend classes. I downloaded the material and made myself practice a few hours every 2 or 3 days for 3 weeks and was successful on my first trial. I was able to get an average of 7.5 and I was aiming at 7."
- *Oswaldo from Venezuela*

High Scorer's Choice IELTS Books

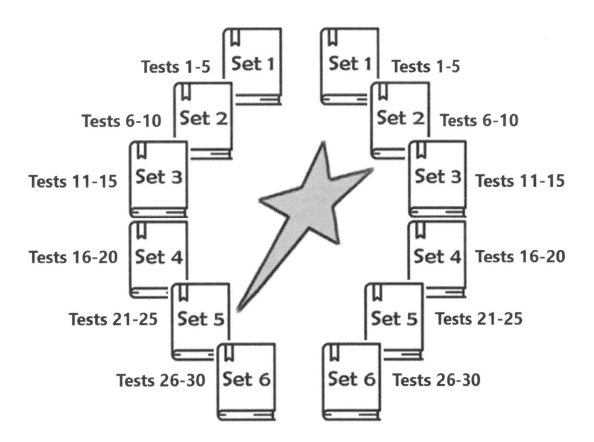

Academic

Tests 1-5 Set 1
Tests 6-10 Set 2
Tests 11-15 Set 3
Tests 16-20 Set 4
Tests 21-25 Set 5
Tests 26-30 Set 6

General

Set 1 Tests 1-5
Set 2 Tests 6-10
Set 3 Tests 11-15
Set 4 Tests 16-20
Set 5 Tests 21-25
Set 6 Tests 26-30

CONTENTS

Download Audio Content

In order to download the audio content please use a desktop computer (not a mobile device) with a reliable internet connection and open the following webpage in your browser:

https://www.ielts-blog.com/ielts-practice-tests-downloads/

Follow instructions on the webpage to save all audio files on your computer. The files are in mp3 format and you will need an audio player to listen to them (any modern computer has that type of software preinstalled).

How to prepare for IELTS

There are two ways for you to use these practice tests for your exam preparation. You can either use them to work on your technique and strategy for each IELTS skill, or you can use them to simulate a real exam and make sure you will do well under time pressure.

Option 1   Use practice tests to work on your IELTS skills (no time limits)

To prepare well for the IELTS exam you need to have a strategy for each sub-test (Listening, Reading, Writing and Speaking). This means knowing what actions to take, and in which order, when you receive a test paper. If you are working with the IELTS self-study book "Ace the IELTS – How to Maximize Your Score", all the necessary tips are located in the book. You need to read and then apply these tips and techniques when you are practicing on some of these tests. Don't time yourself, concentrate on learning the techniques and making sure they work for you.

If you purchased the practice tests in digital format, you will need to print out some pages, for easier learning and to be able to work in the same way as in the real test (on paper). Print the Listening questions and the Reading passages and questions. You can read the Writing and Speaking questions from your computer or mobile device, to save paper and ink. If you have the paperback format, this doesn't apply to you. Use Table of Contents on the previous page to navigate this book.

If Listening is one of your weaker skills, use audio transcripts while listening to recordings, when you hear words or sentences that you don't understand. Stop the recording, rewind, locate in the transcript the sentence you had a problem with, read it, and then listen to the recording again. In the audio transcripts the sentences with answers are underlined for easy learning.

If Reading is hard for you, after doing the Reading test use the Reading Answer Help section of these practice tests to understand why the answers in the Answer key are correct. It will show you the exact locations of the answers in the Reading passages.

To compare your own writing to high-scoring samples go to Example Writing Answers and read them. Note the way the information is grouped and the tone (formal/informal) used in Writing Task 1, and the way an essay is organised in Writing Task 2.

To practice in Speaking, either read to yourself the Speaking test questions or get a friend to help with that. Record your answers and then listen to the recording. Note where you make long pauses while searching for the right word, pay attention to your errors and your pronunciation. Compare your own performance to that of students in sample interviews, and read their Examiner's reports.

Option 2   Use practice tests to simulate the real test (strict time limits)

This option will require some prep work before you can start a simulated test. Print out or photocopy the blank Test Answer Sheets for Listening and Reading and prepare some ruled paper on which to write your Writing Task 1 and 2. Also, think of a way to record yourself in the Speaking sub-test. Get a watch, preferably with a timer. Allocate 3 hours of uninterrupted time.

1. Be in a quiet room, put the Listening questions in front of you and start playing the recording. Answer questions as you listen, and write your answers next to the questions in the book.

2. When the recording has finished playing, allocate 10 minutes to transfer all your Listening answers to the Listening Answer Sheet. While you are transferring the answers check for spelling or grammatical errors and if you missed an answer, write your best guess.

3. Put the Reading passages and questions in front of you and set the timer to 60 minutes. Begin reading passages and answering questions. You can write the answers next to the questions or straight on the Answer Sheet. Remember that you don't get extra time to copy answers to the Answer Sheet, and that when 60 minutes are up all your answers must be written on the Answer Sheet.

4. Put the Writing questions in front of you and set the timer to 60 minutes. Make sure you don't use more than 20 minutes for Task 1, including proofreading time, and that you don't use more than 40 minutes for Task 2, with proofreading included.

5. Put the Speaking questions in front of you and begin the interview (remember to record your answers). In Part 2 take the whole 1 minute to prepare your speech and make notes, and then try to speak for 2 minutes (set the timer before you start talking).

6. When you have finished the whole test, take some time to rest, as you may be tired and it may be hard for you to concentrate. Then check your answers in the Listening and Reading against the correct ones in the Answer key, compare your writing tasks to the Example Writing tasks and your recorded speaking to the example interview. Analyse and learn from any mistakes you may find, and especially notice any problems with time management you may have encountered.

    Remember, it is OK to make mistakes while practicing as long as you are learning from them and improving with every test you take.

    Good luck with your exam preparation!

PRACTICE TEST 11

LISTENING

Download audio recordings for the test here:
https://www.ielts-blog.com/ielts-practice-tests-downloads/

PART 1   *Questions 1 – 10*

Questions 1 – 5

Complete the sentences below.

*Write **NO MORE THAN THREE WORDS AND/OR A NUMBER** from the listening for each answer.*

1   Louise's last bus pass began _6 months_ ago.

2   Louise now wants to be contacted by _email_.

3   Unlike her previous bus pass, Louise's new one will have a _Photo_ on it.

4   The new bus pass has gone up in price by _5 %_.

5   Louise has to put her _Signature_ on her bus pass to make it valid.

Questions 6 – 8

Match the bus stops (questions 6 - 8) with their locations (A - H).

Write the correct letter (A - H) next to questions 6 - 8.

BUS STOPS

North town hall

6	Bus Stop Q	_E_
7	Bus Stop G	A
8	Bus Stop A	G

LOCATIONS

A	West Gate Shopping Centre
B	West Howe
C	The University
D	The Town Centre Post Office
E	The Town Hall
F	The Hospital
(G)	The Arrowdown Sports Centre
H	The Cinema

Questions 9 and 10

Choose TWO letters, A - E.

Which TWO of the following will Louise get discounts on prices with her bus pass?

A ✓   The cinema

(B)   Local train services

C   The local football club

(D)   The local theatre

E   The local museum

PART 2   *Questions 11 - 20*

Questions 11 – 15

Answer the questions below.

*Write **NO MORE THAN THREE WORDS AND/OR A NUMBER** from the listening for each answer.*

11   Which organisation founded the adult education centre?

Town council

12   How often is the teaching of the adult education centre's teachers assessed?

6 - months

13   Where can all the lesson resources be found online?

the interactive classroom

14   How long is one of the teachers' weekly online tutorial sessions?

3 hrs

15   At what time does the administration section in Langdon Street close to the general public?

to 5pm   2 PM

Questions 16 – 20

Complete the table below on the courses that the Adult Education Centre offers.

Write **NO MORE THAN THREE WORDS** from the listening for each answer.

Course	Notes
Languages	* European languages and others. * For different abilities assessment * A (**16**) _Self assesment_ available on the website.
Business	* Short 1-day courses or longer ones to gain a qualification. * Computer software, (**17**) _____, search engine optimisation and website development. * Most popular courses. * Only 10 people a course so book quickly.
Photography and (**18**) _____ computers Photography	* How to get the most from your camera. * Basic to advanced courses - build up knowledge and learn about your equipment.
Cooking ~~foolard~~ shortcuts	* Speciality or the popular introduction to cooking. * Basics and some more advanced topics covered. * Learn all about store cupboard ingredients. * Learn important techniques. * (**19**) _____ for fast and fun cooking.
Creative Writing	* Course run by studying practical exercises with discussion and examples. * Gives an insight to the creative process. * Hopeful writers can learn the (**20**) _____ for creating fiction. techniques
Check the website for details of other courses.	

Page 10

PART 3   Questions 21 – 30

Questions 21 – 26

Complete the table below on events related to the students' survey mentioned in the listening.

Write **NO MORE THAN TWO WORDS** from the listening for each answer.

Survey on Community Benefits from the Digital Environment		
Topic Number	Topic	Notes
1	Perceptions of Internet Speed	(**21**) _broadband_, not dial-up
2	Perceptions of Affordability	Avoid questions related to travel to avoid creating (**22**) _bias_ in the answers
3	Changing Subscriptions and Providers	Focus on locked in contracts and length of (**23**) _term_
4	Transparency Regarding (**24**) _tariff_	Very topical; Communication companies look for the best (**25**) _profit_ from a deal rather than their customers' financial well-being
5	Mobile Phones - users' satisfaction with receiving their (**26**) _signal reception_	Topical again; other countries better than this country

Questions 27 and 28

*Circle the correct letters **A - C**.*

27   When will the four students conduct their survey?

      A   Wednesday afternoon
      B   Friday afternoon
      (C)   Saturday afternoon

28   Where is the final decision to conduct the survey?

      (A)   The town centre
      B   The train station
      C   The central shopping mall

Questions 29 and 30

Complete the sentences below.

*Write **NO MORE THAN TWO WORDS** from the listening for each answer.*

29   Abbie suggests that the group meets the next day to collate the survey's results and perform some _____ on them. *statistical analysis*

30   Martin's trip to the _____ prevents him meeting the others on Sunday evening. *cinema*

PART 4   Questions 31 – 40

Questions 31 - 37

Complete the notes below on geothermal energy and Iceland.

*Write **NO MORE THAN THREE WORDS AND/OR A NUMBER** from the listening for each answer.*

Geothermal Energy and Iceland

* Geothermal energy is heat from the Earth
* Found underground; sometimes shallow, sometimes deep (to the magma layer)
* Most of the energy comes from the (**31**) _____ of radioactive minerals (ie: uranium and potassium)   *decay*

* Iceland at the forefront of geothermal energy for heating and electricity production (currently it supplies 25% of the country's electricity production)
* 84% of energy use is from domestic renewable resources (66% is geothermal)
* In the 20th century, Iceland changed from a poor country to one with a high (**32**) _____   *Standard of living*

* Iceland is on a geological fault line
* The North American and Eurasian tectonic plates move at (**33**) _2_ cm annually
* Creates a lot of volcanic activity and regular (**34**) _____ (not usually dangerous)   *earthquakes*
* Lots of volcanoes (more than 200) and hot springs
* Approx. 30 volcanoes have erupted since Iceland was populated

* Iceland's geothermal energy comes from 2 types of hot water systems:

1   High Temperature Fields
     Found in the (**35**) _____ or nearby   *active volcanic zones*
     Usually at altitude
     The rock is young and permeable
     Groundwater is deep
     Shown at surface usually as outlets for (**36**) _____   *steam vents*

2   Low Temperature Fields
     Found usually in southwest Iceland
     Shown at surface usually as hot or boiling springs
     Flow rates from almost zero to 180 litres a second   *transient*
     These fields are thought to be (**37**) _____ (existing a few thousand years)

Questions 38 – 40

Complete the diagram below on a geothermal electricity generating plant.

Write **NO MORE THAN THREE WORDS** from the listening for each answer.

A Geothermal Electricity Generating Plant

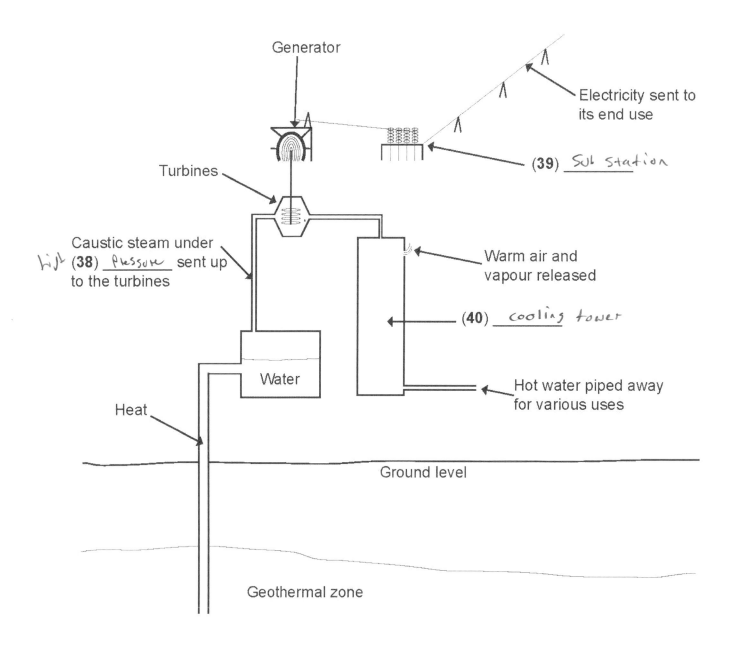

READING

SECTION 1   *Questions 1 – 14*

Questions 1 – 7

*There are 4 advertisements **A – D** on the next page.*

*Answer the questions below by writing the letters of the appropriate advertisements in boxes **1 – 7** on your answer sheet.*

1   Which advertisement says someone can visit customers in their homes?

2   Which advertisement says the business operates internationally?

3   Which advertisement says the business can provide references?

4   Which advertisement says the business will telephone the customer on request?

5   Which advertisement says it does not charge if the project is not successful?

6   Which advertisement says all its charges do not need to be paid straight away?

7   Which advertisement says it can identify problems where customers live?

A   Swales Home Insurance

THE Home Insurer.

- No claims discount available
- Flexible payment options with installments
- FREE accidental cover for audio and desktop computer equipment
- FREE home emergency cover for electrical, gas, drains and plumbing emergencies
- FREE identity theft cover for legal and other fees you may incur
- No house inspection needed

Get wise! Get Swales!

Call 08056 832 776 for an instant on the phone quote!

B   Howard Solicitors

Have you been injured recently and it wasn't your fault?

Call Howard Solicitors for our no win no fee service.

We can assess your injury and plan how to get you compensation without any stress or hassle on your part. Any medical examinations can be done in local clinics and you probably won't even need to step inside a courtroom.

We have hundreds of genuine, satisfied customers who you can contact to hear about our professional service.

Set up a free 1st consultation to discuss your case today on: 05381 888 333.

C   GLENCHAPEL STOCKBROKERS

Do you want to invest in stocks, shares, bonds and currencies around the world? Glenchapel provides an unparalleled service to help you. We can provide advice and predictions regarding market trends and affective factors to help you make the best choices to ensure your money grows. We can handle all purchase or sell orders or you can do it yourself on our online investment platform. We charge no commission and our buy - sell prices are the most competitive in the market. We specialise in the US, UK, China, Australia and Canada markets, but we have opportunities from all around the world. Check us out today on our website and book an online or call-back consultation with one of our investment executives.

www.glenchapel.com

D   Steve Johnson & Associates
Architectural Consultants and Surveyors

Commercial & Residential, Construction, Barn Conversions, Alterations & Extensions

* Architectural Design and Alterations
* Local Authority Planning Applications
* Rural and Historical Buildings
* Planning and Development

* Building Surveys and Reports
* Architectural Drawings
* Building Defect Analysis
* New Builds

Drop into our offices or we can visit you in your house, offices or your project's location.
18 Farm Way, Drawstone, DR6 J87.
www.johnsonassociates.ca

Questions 8 – 14

Do the following statements agree with the information given in the text?

In boxes 8 – 14 on your answer sheet write:

TRUE	*if the statement agrees with the information*
FALSE	*if the statement contradicts the information*
NOT GIVEN	*if there is no information on this*

8 Bournepoint is the largest shopping park in the country.

9 Visitors to Bournepoint cannot currently visit the cinema there.

10 Swimming lessons are available at the leisure centre.

11 It's advised to make a reservation for bowling if people want to play on Saturday evenings.

12 Customers have to pay extra to print things in the Management Centre.

13 Bicycle users are advised to use a smaller bicycle lock to secure their bikes.

14 The car parks are monitored by security during park opening hours.

Bournepoint Shopping Centre

Bournepoint Shopping Park is a unique retail experience. Located on the edge of town, Bournepoint is one of the largest shopping parks in the country and has many of the biggest stores in the region. In addition to the DIY, pet and gardening superstores and three large supermarkets, we are home to dozens of large High Street brands, as well as restaurants and cafés. Next year, the CinePlus Multiplex Cinema will open, allowing you to shop, eat and visit the cinema without needing to travel elsewhere.

ShoppingMobility   ShoppingMobility provides a solution to many of the shopping problems faced by those with impaired mobility. It is available to anyone, young or old, no matter whether their mobility impairment is temporary or permanent, caused by illness, accident, pregnancy or ageing. Powered scooters and wheelchairs are available as well as manual wheelchairs. Using any of the Bournepoint's mobility equipment is completely free and full training can be given on any of the equipment and bookings can be made in advance to ensure availability. First time visitors will be asked to register and will need to show some form of identification.

The Leisure Complex   In our leisure complex, visitors can swim, go bowling, play pool, or take advantage of the town's only laser shooting centre. The leisure complex is open during Bournepoint's usual opening hours and all activities can be booked online or you can just turn up and go for it. The bowling is very popular at weekend evenings, so booking this in advance is a good idea. Bowling lessons are available every day in the afternoons and this can be a fun way to spend an afternoon with your friends or maybe plan as a party for your child. Check things out at the website for more details.

Management Suite   We have a Management Suite available for people to rent office space on a daily or even part-day basis. An office can be rented by just turning up on the day, by telephoning the reservation centre or by using our app. You will be assigned a private room with desk and telephone. There are photocopying, printing, Internet, fax and national telephone services available as part of the price.

Bicycle Security   We are fully aware of the amount of bike theft that occurs locally. Bournepoint Shopping Centre is working with the Police in the community to help prevent the possible theft of your bike. D locks are considered the most secure way to lock up your bike. Large D locks are easier to use and can lock several bikes at a time, but mini D locks are light and easy to carry, plus they are harder for thieves to break. It will give you the peace of mind that you can leave your bike secure when you go shopping.

Bathrooms and Baby Changing   There are two toilet facilities situated at the Bournepoint Shopping Centre. The East Bathrooms are situated next to the Management Suite. The West Bathrooms are situated next to the Multiplex Cinema. Bath bathrooms also have separate parent and baby facilities for changing and feeding. Some individual stores have their own bathrooms available. Please dispose of any baby changing materials in the specialised bins provided.

Parking   We have over 3000 free car-park spaces with late night trading from Mondays to Thursday until 8.00 p.m. and 10 p.m. on Fridays and Saturdays, making Bournepoint a wonderful place to do all your shopping and leisure activities in one convenient location. All facilities on Sunday are open from 10 a.m. and close at 4 p.m. The cinema will have later closing.

SECTION 2   *Questions 15 – 27*

Questions 15 – 20

Complete the summary using the words in the box below.

*Write your answers in boxes **15 - 20** on your answer sheet.*

Dawson's Ltd. - Company In-service Training

Dawson's staff training is available to all staff if it's deemed to be advantageous for both staff and company. A personal development plan will be (**15**) _____ for everyone and reviewed annually. The (**16**) _____ selected for training are chosen by staff. This will help work practices and staff will feel valued and less likely to (**17**) _____. Training applied for will be paid wholly or partly by Dawson's, but the company must be repaid if an employee fails any (**18**) _____ at the training. To apply, employees send the relevant completed form to their line manager, detailing the dates, costs and (**19**) _____ of the training. Various training sessions will soon take place, some of which are (**20**) _____ and some led by other groups.

---

in-house	monthly
improved	annually
assessment	self-study
complain	skills
convenient	participants
attendance	people
resign	tailored
advantageous	relevance
inexpensive	copied

Dawson's Ltd. - Company In-service Training

Here at Dawson's, we believe in continually training our staff, so that they can grow personally and our company can grow as a result. We offer regular training sessions for all our staff and you can also apply for any training specific to yourself that you think could be beneficial to you and the company.

When you join Dawson's, we will create a personal development plan for you. In consultation with you, we will identify your strengths and weaknesses, and take into account the way you like to learn. We will review what we've agreed with you at least once a year to evaluate your progress. At these sessions, you can discuss with your line manager any training that you feel you require.

The Benefits of Dawson's Company Training

Staff training can improve business performance, profit and staff self-esteem. The advantages to Dawson's and you include:

- *you* choose what new abilities you feel you need to improve working for us. You know best how to target abilities to meet the needs of our operation for now and in the future.
- training you can result in better customer service, better work safety practices and productivity improvements.
- we demonstrate to our workforce that we value you enough to invest in you; this can improve staff retention. We hope this makes you as happy as it does us.

Notes on training that you may wish to apply for:

- training needs to be job-related for Dawson's to pay for it
- if the training is useful to Dawson's, but not necessary to someone's job, you'll pay 50% of the course costs and we can pay the rest
- employees must pay us back if they don't complete or pass the course (if evaluation is part of the course)

There is a Training Application Form available on the company website. Fill it in digitally and submit it to your line manager by email. Be careful to include the dates, training fees, any travel or accommodation expenses and how the training applies to you and your role at Dawson's.

Company Training

The following training sessions are coming up for everyone soon:

- Dealing with difficult customers
- Coping with email loads
- Stress – spotting it and how to deal with it
- Health and safety
- Project management

Some of these courses are run by specialists who are already part of our company and others are outsourced to organisations that specialise in the relevant field.

Questions 21 – 27

Complete the sentences below.

Write **NO MORE THAN TWO WORDS** *from the text for each answer.*

Write your answers in boxes **21 - 27** *on your answer sheet.*

21   Creating a green office can improve employee _____ as well as their
         work ethic.

22   _____ in one's personal life can be noticed when improvements in work
         life are implemented.

23   Get someone to check what things your local _____ will take and what they
         won't.

24   There may be _____ governing how you get rid of items containing
         dangerous materials.

25   Try to use _____ from parties rather than just throwing them away.

26   Reflect on the _____ of anything you buy, as longer-lasting things will
         reduce rubbish and save you cash.

27   A _____ between work and the environment can be achieved by turning
         an office green.

Be a Green Office!

Engage and motivate your co-workers to buy green products and help reduce waste. Learn more about how your office can go green!

A green office can mean all sorts of things, ranging from simply decreasing supply purchase and increasing the number of eco-friendly alternatives to the more advanced actions such as switching energy providers and eliminating waste through a variety of means. In addition to all this, a green office can have a significant effect on employees in terms of morale.

Adding a green aspect to the office equation can also help to make members of a team more aware of their actions with regard to the environment, which is fantastic; it may also add to their work ethic as well. Paying closer attention to details in one aspect of life can lead to recognising shortcomings in others. Subsequently, employees on board with the benefits of a green office can become more well-rounded individuals that respect the environment, indoors and out, and their co-workers that much more.

Here are some examples of what you can do:

- Recycle office paper, newspapers, beverage containers, electronic equipment and batteries. Contact a nearby recycling facility and establish what materials they accept.
- Consider using safer alternatives to common and potentially hazardous chemicals used in products and processes.
- For businesses, there may be regulations on the disposal of electronics, batteries and mercury-containing lamps, as they may contain hazardous substances.
- To help reduce waste, use two-sided printing and copying, buy supplies made with recycled content, and top up any printer cartridges you use rather than purchasing fresh replacements – it's cheaper and greener!
- Before replacing a computer that no longer fits your needs, investigate enhancing its capacity. Many modifications can be made with little know-how using the help of the manufacturer or a do-it-yourself guide.
- When purchasing new electronics, consider a leasing program that includes proper reuse and recycling.
- After office festivities, put leftovers in recyclable containers, and share them with family, friends, or others. Donate whole, untouched leftovers from parties to a local food bank or homeless shelter.
- Purchase office supplies in bulk or multi-packs to diminish packaging waste. You can also buy items with packaging that can be reused or recycled.
- Buy energy-efficient items in the office when buying electronics, such as computers.
- Consider the durability of a product before you purchase it. Cheaper, less durable items often wear out quickly, creating waste and costing you money. Look for items that embody the concept of reuse.

Office culture doesn't have to be at odds with the outside world and taking eco options can help employees feel more relaxed, welcomed and thus happier. Green offices connect the business aspect of life to the natural world, which in turn can help to create a symbiosis between the two. Connecting with the natural world by decreasing consumption and opting for friendlier options can help us to understand the true reasons behind our decisions.

SECTION 3   *Questions 28 – 40*

Read the following passage and answer Questions 28 – 40.

The Search for Life in Outer Space

Ever since the human mind has been able to think outside the box and the extent of outer space has gradually become known, the question of whether we are alone or not has fascinated us. The possibility of a different type of life, in imaginable or unimaginable forms, has shaped **scientific research** and the development of different cultures and traditions around the world.

When Galileo Galilei, an Italian astronomer, first detected Mars with a primitive telescope in 1609, mankind was, for the first time, confronted with the idea that planet Earth was probably not the centre of the universe. Other planets, even greater than Earth, possibly dominated the space around us. Astronomer Schiaparelli's observations two hundred and seventy years later resulted in a superficial map of Mars' surface being constructed, containing linear features. These, Schiaparelli said, hinted at waterways, possibly created by an intelligent race. Even though these observations were later discarded and described as an **optical illusion**, the hope of another form of life on Mars was not completely given up until the 1960's, when NASA's Mariner spacecraft landed on Mars and finally provided photographs and scientific evidence that gave proof of the uninhabitable nature of Earth's red neighbour. However, when the idea of life in outer space is discussed, Mars is often still brought up as one of the first subjects, and this is possibly due to its early discovery in mankind's search of the universe around us.

A study released recently reports that ancient Mars harboured a form of nitrogen that could potentially have been used by microbes, if any existed, to build key molecules, such as amino acids. Bored samples from a sedimentary mudstone had previously allowed Mars-rover team members to conclude that, billions of years ago, the area was part of a potentially life-supporting lake-and-stream system. The discovery of fixed nitrogen contributes to this habitability picture. This, however, is not the kind of life that people often think about. People want discovery of an intelligent life, not a tiny microbe.

Today, different projects and organisations have tried to shed light on the controversial issue of intelligent life in outer space. The SETI organisation, the Search for Extra-Terrestrial Intelligence and the largest organisation of its kind, has not seen any success in the past fifty years. Even though this does not eliminate the possibility of other forms of life, it does imply that if they do exist, they do so far from our reach, and these distances complicate any advances in the field. Radio messages and light impulses are seen as methods to communicate with other races, and SETI as well as other organisations and research facilities operate and have operated with these signals. It is likely that lasers will be developed to exploit their even greater range within a few years.

In the past, several attempts to communicate and give evidence of our existence have been made, though without notable success. The "Wow Signal" is regarded as being an exception. It was a signal picked up by a telescope at an American university in 1977 and appeared to have all the right characteristics to have originated from an intelligent species. The fact that no signal was ever received from the same area of the sky again led to the event being regarded as a coincidence or a misinterpretation. However, attempts to communicate and make ourselves known through signals sent to space are now handled with caution. The opinion that this may bring a threat to mankind's existence is not as abstract as it has been presented in many science fiction movies, and scientists as well as astronomers are reluctant to pursue active signalling. It should also be considered that several conditions would need to be present in order for success to occur. Firstly, the extra-terrestrial species would need to have similar technological facilities to ours. Secondly, they would want to make themselves become known, which may not be the case. Thirdly, and most importantly though, they would need to exist in the same era as us, which, considering the large time spans of the universe, is quite unlikely.

Due to technological restrictions, the search for extra-terrestrial life has, for the time being, been limited to our own and some parts of nearby solar systems. Evidence of water vapour and ozone in the atmosphere of another planet are good conditions for most forms of life to exist and are therefore key elements that scientists try to research and identify in order to describe a planet as inhabitable. Even though some people argue that the conditions humans need to survive should not necessarily be the same for other forms of life, it is logical to conclude that these conditions are likely to be needed by another race, as the universe uses a similar chemistry. However, due to the fact that the development from one-celled organisms to several-celled ones is very unlikely and the emergence of intelligence is even more unlikely, many renowned scientists are now less optimistic and are convinced that, at present, we are the only intelligent species in this galaxy.

The new and unknown has always fascinated us, and this is why scientists, astronomers and organisations like the SETI refuse to give up the search. The chances of success are difficult to estimate and probably low, but if no attempts are made, the chance of a discovery is zero.

Questions 28 – 35

Complete the notes below.

*Write **NO MORE THAN TWO WORDS** for each answer.*

*Write your answers in boxes **28 - 35** on your answer sheet.*

The History and Role of Mars in the Search for Life

* The chances of finding alien life forms has influenced (**28**) _____ and how societies have developed their way of life.
* In 1609, Galileo Galilei's early use of a primitive telescope led to his discovery of Mars.
* It became questionable whether Earth is the centre of the universe - rejected as being an optical illusion.
* The creation of a map of Mars' surface with what one astronomer thought were (**29**) _____ brought up the idea of a civilisation on Mars.
* NASA's Mariner spacecraft finally proved that Mars was (**30**) _____.
* Mars is still a common subject when discussing alien life.

Recent Discoveries on Mars

* A certain type of nitrogen used to make amino acids and microbes has been found in mudstone (**31**) _____ drilled by the Mars-rover.
* The discovery has led to conclusions of ancient lakes and streams on Mars.
* Not the type of extra-terrestrial being usually imagined.

Research Organisations and Signalling

* The search for intelligent life in outer space is still regarded as (**32**) _____.
* The possibility of other forms of life is not impossible, but the great (**33**) _____, make communication difficult.
* Radio messages and light impulses have been used in the past.
* In the near future, (**34**) _____ will probably be used, as they will have a better (**35**) _____.

Questions 36 – 38

Do the following statements agree with the information given in the text?

In boxes 36 – 38 on your answer sheet write:

> **TRUE**   *if the statement agrees with the information*
> **FALSE**   *if the statement contradicts the information*
> **NOT GIVEN**   *if there is no information on this*

36   The "Wow Signal" was rejected as alien contact, as it was believed to be the result of deliberate manipulation by a research member.

37   Scientists are confident to continue signalling, as the danger of this process for Earth and its inhabitants is regarded to be non-existent.

38   Active signalling on a continuous basis is necessary in order to obtain possible answers from races of outer space.

Questions 39 and 40

*Choose the correct letter **A, B, C or D**.*

*Write the correct letter in boxes **39 and 40** on your answer sheet.*

39   The key condition to finding intelligent life in the universe is

A   that it would have to use similar technology to us.
B   that it would want to be found.
C   that it would have to be in a galaxy near enough to travel to.
D   it would have to live in the same time period as us.

40   Scientists are now less optimistic that extra-terrestrial intelligent life exists, because

A   the universe uses a complex chemistry for its basic functions.
B   intelligence is hardly measurable.
C   the conversion from single cells to multiple cells is not probable.
D   if it were there, we'd have found it already.

WRITING

WRITING TASK 1

You should spend about 20 minutes on this task.

> **You recently moved to a new house and you want to invite an old friend to stay with you.**
>
> **Write a letter to your friend. In your letter,**
>
> - **invite him to stay and suggest a date** ✓
> - **briefly describe the new house and garden**
> - **say why you like your new house**

You should write at least 150 words.

*You do **NOT** need to write any addresses. Begin your letter as follows:*

> ***Dear Jimmy,***

WRITING TASK 2

You should spend about 40 minutes on this task.

Write about the following topic:

> **Should governments or teachers be responsible for what is to be taught in schools?**

Give reasons for your answer and include any relevant examples from your knowledge or experience.

You should write at least 250 words.

SPEAKING

PART 1

- Can you describe your old school to me?
- How did you get to school every day?
- Did you enjoy your experience at school? (Why/Why not?)

Topic 1   The Seasons

- Which is your favourite season?
- What sports are popular in different seasons in your country?
- In which season do you think it's best to get married?
- What problems are caused by extreme seasonal weather?

Topic 2   Languages

- Is the language in your country difficult to learn?
- What languages are learned at schools in your country?
- What are the advantages of speaking more than one language?
- When you visit a foreign country, do you try and learn some of the language? (Why/Why not?)

PART 2

Describe a sport or game that you like to watch or play.
You should say:
         why you like to watch or play this sport or game
         where you watch or play this sport or game
         how much it costs to watch or play this sport or game
and briefly explain how the game is played.

PART 3

Topic 1   Exercise and Health

- Why is doing exercise good for you?
- How can we get young people to exercise more?
- How can sport improve people's mental health?
- How can sport be bad for your health?

Topic 2   Sport and Money

- How have trends in sport changed over the last 50 years?
- Do you think that top sportsmen and women are sometimes overpaid? (Why/Why not?)
- How do you feel about betting and sport?
- How important is the relationship between sport and advertising?

PRACTICE TEST 12

LISTENING

 Download audio recordings for the test here:
https://www.ielts-blog.com/ielts-practice-tests-downloads/

PART 1   *Questions 1 – 10*

Questions 1 – 5

*Circle the correct letters **A - C**.*

1   Graham and Sophie's first night in Oban is on the

     A   7th July.
     B   8th July.
     C   13th July.

2   Graham and Sophie plan to travel to Oban by

     A   car.
     B   bus.
     C   train.

3   Sophie said that she'd check places to stay in, but

     A   she only ordered some magazines.
     B   she didn't do anything.
     C   she only checked a few things on the internet.

4   In Oban, Graham and Sophie will stay

     A   in a hostel.
     B   in a guest house.
     C   in a hotel.

5   Graham and Sophie's booking for accommodation will include

     A   breakfast but not dinner.
     B   breakfast and dinner.
     C   neither breakfast nor dinner.

Questions 6 – 10

Complete Sophie's table notes below on her hiking holiday.

*Write **NO MORE THAN ONE WORD OR A NUMBER** from the listening for each answer.*

	Hike 1	Hike 2
Where	Oban to Dunbeg	Island of Kerrera
Difficulty	Easy (no (**6**) _Hills_)	Easy
Distance	Along coast for 3½ hours	About (**8**) _5_ miles in length
Sights	The sea, island of Kerrera, cathedral and a spectacular ruined castle	Land and some sea views; castle
Notes	Lunch in Dunbeg and then take a (**7**) _Bus_ home (around 15 minutes)	Go slowly - look around the castle and have a (**9**) _picknic_
We can buy a (**10**) _Map_ on the ferry.		

PART 2   Questions 11 - 20

Questions 11 and 12

Choose **TWO** letters, **A - F**.

Where did the money come from to buy the town's new museum's building?

A   from the local Weyport town council

B   from money collected from the general public

C   from the previous town museum

D   from the previous museum director

E   from a local business

F   from the central arts council

Questions 13 – 15

Choose **THREE** letters, **A - G**.

What has the town's new museum's building been used for since it was built?

A   An office building

B   The fire service

C   An insurance company

D   Keeping council property

E   An army centre

F   The council education department

G   The council housing department

Questions 16 – 20

*Below is a plan of the Weyport Museum ground floor with **9** locations marked **A - I**.*
*Questions **16 - 20** name **5** things that can be seen or visited in the museum.*
*Write the correct letter (**A - I**) that matches the things with their locations.*

16   The bathrooms   D

17   Paintings   B

18   Silverware   C

19   Film   H

20   Toys   A

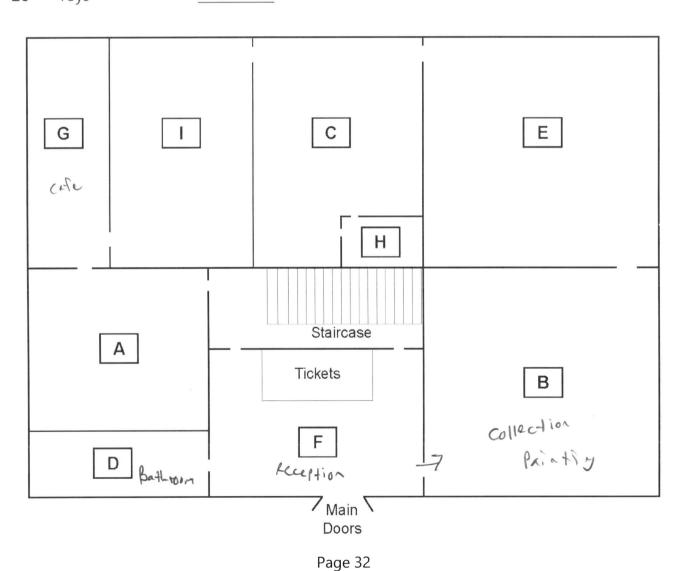

PART 3   *Questions 21 – 30*

Questions 21 – 25

Complete the flow chart that summarises the students' planning of their field trip.

*Choose **FIVE** answers from the list below (**A - H**) and write the correct letter next to questions **21 - 25**.*

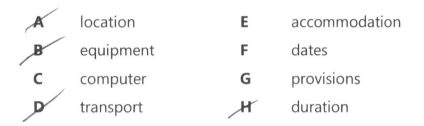

A	location	E	accommodation
B	equipment	F	dates
C	computer	G	provisions
D	transport	H	duration

Cliff Formation Survey Field Trip

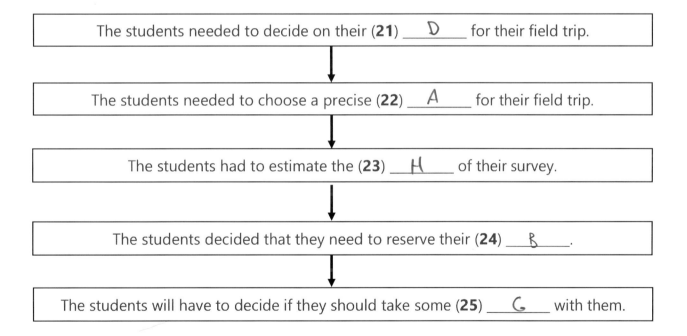

The students needed to decide on their (**21**) __D__ for their field trip.

↓

The students needed to choose a precise (**22**) __A__ for their field trip.

↓

The students had to estimate the (**23**) __H__ of their survey.

↓

The students decided that they need to reserve their (**24**) __B__ .

↓

The students will have to decide if they should take some (**25**) __G__ with them.

Questions 26 – 28

Complete the diagram below on the students' target area of coastal cliff erosion.

*Write **NO MORE THAN TWO WORDS** from the listening for each answer.*

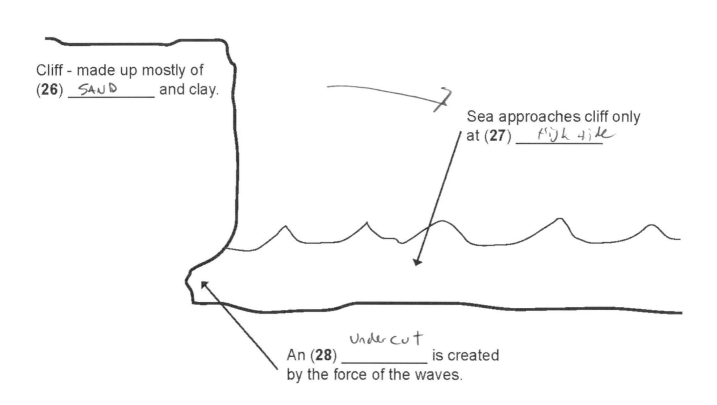

Cliff - made up mostly of
(26) _SAND_ and clay.

Sea approaches cliff only
at (27) _High tide_

An (28) _Undercut_ is created
by the force of the waves.

Questions 29 and 30

Answer the questions below.

*Write **NO MORE THAN TWO WORDS** from the listening for each answer.*

29   Which organisation monitors the coastal cliff erosion where the students will be going?

      Coast guard

30   What does Alan say the students should bring in case they run into any danger?

      Mobile Phones

PART 4   *Questions 31 – 40*

Questions 31 – 40

Complete the summary below on the lecture on the Wechsler-Belleview Intelligence Scale.

Write **NO MORE THAN TWO WORDS** *from the listening for each answer.*

The Wechsler-Belleview Intelligence Scale (The WBIS)

Wechsler believed intelligence was made up of different skills considered within the context of the complete (**31**) _____. His intelligence scale broke away from existing intelligence tests and set up a numerical scale with the (**32**) _____ set at 100.
arbitrary

Wechsler decided to create a test to measure these different skills that made up intelligence. The 2 main areas tested were (**33**) *verbal* and performance and these were then broken down to 14 sub-tests, 7 for each. These 14 topics remain the basis for today's WBIS, which is today's most commonly used (**34**) _____ assessment.

The WBIS is aimed at adults; for younger children other related scales are used, neither of which need (**35**) _____ in a child.

The WBIS is not suitable for assessing the (**36**) _____ of intelligence or of the age range. For any of these situations, care should be taken with the (**37**) _____ of the results.

brain damage
The WBIS can also be used for neuropsychological assessment. Differences in answers can indicate types of (**38**) _____. In addition, the WBIS is used to diagnose learning disabilities and ADHD. Although experts say the WBIS is best used only for intelligence, it is used to compare cognitive development and performance in social skills or at (**39**) *School*.
best

The WBIS is highly regarded as an intelligence test and is often used as a point of comparison for other tests when assessing their (**40**) _____ and validity.
studies

READING

SECTION 1   Questions 1 – 14

Questions 1 – 6

Complete the sentences below.

*Write **NO MORE THAN TWO WORDS** from the text for each answer.*

*Write your answers in boxes **1 - 6** on your answer sheet.*

1   Having a friend nearby just before an operation can help reduce _____.

2   A pre-operative assessment may be conducted face to face, by phone or by _____.

3   Part of a pre-operative assessment might include a test of a patient's _____.

4   Patients might be told to stop their normal _____ in their pre-operative assessment.

5   Patients might suffer negative effects if they eat or drink before their pre-operative _____ is administered.

6   Removing all cosmetics allows doctors to properly assess a patient's _____.

What to do Before an Operation in Hospital

For most people, an operation is a worrying event, regardless of the procedure or whether they have had surgery before. Being organised and prepared for your operation can help alleviate some of the stressful feelings. In the days leading up to your surgery, you'll need to think about how you'll get to the hospital and back again. You probably won't be well enough to drive, so you may want to arrange transport or ask a friend or relative to help. Make sure you give your family and friends plenty of notice about your operation, so that if necessary they can take time off work to be with you. The most difficult time is waiting for the surgery. If possible, having someone to sit with you before it takes place - perhaps a relative or a friend - may help to diminish anxiety. Check your hospital's policy on visiting times and let your family and friends know. When preparing your things for your stay, remember to bring your appointment card with you too.

Pre-operative assessment

At some hospitals, you'll be asked to attend a pre-operative assessment, which may be an appointment with a nurse or doctor, a telephone assessment or an email assessment. You'll be asked questions about your health, your medical history and your home circumstances. If the assessment involves a visit to the hospital, some tests may be carried out, including a blood test. This assessment will usually happen one or more days before your operation. Make sure you know the results of any previous tests. You'll be given clear information on the following:

- if you need to fast in the hours before your operation (see below)
- whether you should cease taking your usual medications before going into hospital
- the overnight things you'll need to bring with you
- whether you'll need to stay in hospital overnight and, if so, for how long

What to Bring

Apart from your overnight things, if you're staying in hospital, you may wish to pack books or magazines, a small amount of money, some healthy snacks and an address book with important phone numbers, including your GP's contact details. Different hospitals tend to have different rules concerning personal electronic equipment. You may want to check with your hospital about their policies on the use of mobile phones, MP3 players and laptops/tablets during your hospital stay.

The importance of fasting

If your doctor has instructed you to fast before the operation, it's really important that you don't eat or drink anything – this includes light snacks, sweets and water. You need an empty stomach during surgery, so you don't vomit while you're under anaesthetic.

Hygiene

You'll need to remove all make-up and nail polish before your operation, as the hospital staff will need to see your skin and nails to make sure your blood circulation is healthy. This can also help to reduce the chances of unwanted bacteria being brought into the hospital.

Questions 7 – 11

Complete the notes below.

Write **NO MORE THAN TWO WORDS** for each answer.

Write your answers in boxes **7 - 11** on your answer sheet.

What to do When Moving Home

* Use a (**7**) _____ to help you remember what to do when moving home.

* Wait until your dwelling sale or rental contracts are completed before informing anyone of your new address.

* Speak to neighbours about the parking of the removal van on the day of the move.

* Organise enough clean clothes for the move duration. Insurance issues stops movers disconnecting washing machines, so book a plumber.

* In order to pay the right (**8**) _____, contact the rates office.

* You might need a new doctor and dentist if you've moved area.

* A form on the Post Office website can allow you to (**9**) _____ your post to the right destination.

* Contact organisations that bill you at your old address. For gas and electricity, make a note of the reading of the old and new properties' (**10**) _____, so that you pay the correct amount. Choose the appropriate organisations and tell them of your new address.

* Check the availability of your new keys and leave your old ones somewhere obvious, but not in sight from a (**11**) _____.

* Tell the DVA of your new address change (and name if relevant).

What to do When Moving Home

There is so much to organise in just packing for the move that important things are often overlooked. Take advantage of a checklist to make sure you've got everything covered. It's best not to tell anyone of your address change until the contracts have been exchanged, otherwise if the sale or rental agreement falls through, you will need to contact everyone again. When the contract is ready, you will need to tell many organisations of your new address.

Liaise with your neighbours about parking before the day of your move. Most people use a removal firm to help them and the average removal van is the same size as a double decker bus. You need to leave room for this lorry to manoeuvre into position. The removal team will usually want to have the back doors of the wagon as near to the access point as possible and if on an incline the lorry will want to be facing downhill (this stops everything falling out when they open the doors).

Make sure you have plenty of clean clothes in accessible places for the duration of your move, so plan some late laundry. After that you might need to arrange for a plumber to disconnect the washing machine. Some removal companies will do this for you but most will not and cannot as they do not have the insurance to do so.

Contact your local rates office to let them know the date you move out of your current property and when you move into your new one, so they bill you correctly for council tax. If you've changed area, you may need to register with a new doctor's surgery (GP) or dentist. If you use other local medical services, don't forget to find alternatives to replace your old ones when you move.

A lot of people and organisations will not know you have changed address and they will continue to send you mail to your old address. To deal with this, redirect your mail to your new address. You can download a form from the Post Office website. It can take up to 10 days to set up and there is a charge.

You don't want to keep paying bills at your old address, so you need to contact the appropriate organisations to stop that. Common bills will apply to the telephone, the gas and electricity providers. You need to tell them at least 48 hours before you are moving. Pass on the details of your current supplier to the people moving in. On your moving day, you will need to read the meters in both dwellings, so the right bills can be issued. When you move in to your new home, contact the companies that you want to deliver your utilities, so they can register you as a new customer and start billing you from that day.

Plan what to do with keys. Please check that the keys to your new home are going to be available and that you know what to do with your own keys. Any spare keys should be clearly labeled and left where they will be seen when you leave the house on moving day. Don't leave them in direct view of any window. The kitchen work top is usually good as it's normally the first room the new people will head towards and organise first.

A lot of official documents are registered to you at your old address, including those to do with driving. You must tell the Driver and Vehicle Agency (DVA) immediately of any changes to your name, address or both. You must also tell the DVA if either the name and address details shown on the registration certificate are incorrect. Make sure as well that you pack valuables and documents and put them in a safe place.

Questions 12 – 14

Do the following statements agree with the information given in the text?

In boxes 12 – 14 on your answer sheet write:

> **TRUE**   *if the statement agrees with the information*
> **FALSE**   *if the statement contradicts the information*
> **NOT GIVEN**   *if there is no information on this*

12   Two projects will be carried out at the same time during the upcoming road works.

13   Alternative bus services will be free of charge during the disturbances.

14   People will not be able to use South Street in phase 4.

Advance Notice of Upcoming Road Works

Sections of the East High Street will be closed from Monday, April 6, for up to 12 weeks to allow for Campion Gas to replace and reinforce gas networks. Your local council is taking the closure as an opportunity to carry out street lighting improvements at the same time so as to minimise possible future disruption.

Campion Gas will carry out the work in four phases:

Phase 1: Broad Avenue, from the roundabout to the junction with Winton Street, will be closed as well as one lane on the Market Square. An alternative route will be available via East High Street, Winton Street and Castle Road.
Phases 2 & 3: East High Street, from the crossroads at Broad Avenue to the junction with Winton Street, will be closed, as will the junction at Winton Street. An alternative route will be available via Winton Street, Castle Road and Broad Avenue.
Phase 4: Eastern Road will be closed from the junction with South Street and No. 15 on that road. One lane only on South Street will also be closed. Exact details of the closures, including dates for each phase, are still to be finalised and will be released in due course.

Your local council website provides details on all the road works, any changes to the above information, how the works affect local public transport routes and timetable and updates on progress.

SECTION 2   *Questions 15 – 27*

Questions 15 – 20

Answer the questions below.

Write **NO MORE THAN THREE WORDS** *from the text for each answer.*

*Write your answers in boxes **15 - 20** on your answer sheet.*

15   What is the principal challenge for the company with having homeworkers?

16   Dealing with which emotion can be a challenge for homeworkers?

17   What do homeworkers perceive they are missing out on the most when they are away from the office?

18   What will the decision depend on if a worker wishes to work part-time as well as working from home?

19   What process will have to take place before an employee can begin working from home?

20   What is often inadequate in people's home offices?

Working from Home - Notes for Employees

The number of employees working from home in office-type jobs, or roles involving travel, where home is used as a base, is steadily increasing. We have therefore published these notes about working for us from home.

Homeworking can present challenges to both you and us. For us, the main issue is the staff management of those who work on their own and away from the main business base. For you, it can include overcoming loneliness and managing the boundaries between home and work life. Often, being away from the managers who are responsible for promotion is felt to be the greatest disadvantage.

Home working can include:

- Working entirely at home apart from attending regular or occasional meetings at the office or with customers
- Time split between office and home or with customers - for example, two days in the office and three days at home or with customers
- Working mainly in the office and working from home only occasionally

Homeworking can also be used in conjunction with other arrangements, such as flexible hours, working part-time, term-time working or working our core hours. The employee's post will determine whether this is possible.

While homeworking can be seen as an attractive option, it will not suit everyone. A homeworker needs to be able to cope with working on their own with little supervision. Homeworkers ideally need to be:

- able to spend long periods on their own and be confident working without supervision
- self-disciplined and self-motivated
- able to separate work from home life

As the employer of all our staff, we have a duty of care for all our employees, and the requirements of the health and safety legislation apply to homeworkers. We are responsible for carrying out a risk assessment to check whether the proposed home workplace's ventilation, temperature, lighting, space, chair, desk and computer, or any kind of workstation, and floor are suitable for the tasks the homeworker will be carrying out. Employees will have to arrange this with us before they start homeworking. We can also advise you on how to create a comfortable and effective office. For example, even with great natural light in people's home offices, you'll still need additional lighting for darker hours of the day, as overhead house lighting is usually insufficient for work. Also when putting a new desk into a home office, a lot of people kind of reflexively put it right up against the wall in the darkest corner of the room. It's better to move your desk close to the windows, but place it parallel to the panes. This ideal set-up gives you the happiness benefits of natural light, and creates a more inspiring place to work. We'd also advise you on stocking up on office basics, as you don't want to be darting out of the office every few minutes when you need things. You'll need to keep all receipts too, as we will refund you a lot of your work expenses.

Any application for homeworking should be made in writing and sent to your line manager. Any refusal will be accompanied by an explanation and employees can make an appeal if they are not satisfied.

Questions 21 – 27

Complete the summary using the words in the box below.

Write your answers in boxes 21 - 27 on your answer sheet.

Staying Healthy at Work

Workers can improve their health and fitness at work. Avoiding stress is important and (**21**) _____ is better than dealing with it after its arrival. Workers should prioritise work and not over-work. Back pain is a common workplace health problem and is caused in different ways. Workers should stay active, use analgesic if necessary, and avoid (**22**) _____. RSI is a threat and can be caused by poor posture, poor equipment or poor (**23**) _____ with equipment. Sitting badly can also cause problems. Workers should be assessed and take lots of (**24**) _____ if they use a computer a lot.

A long (**25**) _____ and working hours are tiring, but workers can exercise at work in different ways or exercise before or after work or at lunchtimes. Developing (**26**) _____ and getting lighter will help workers in all areas of health. As people eat a lot at work, how they eat affects their health and (**27**) _____. Avoidance of lunch or eating while working is not healthy – people should exploit the lunch break to feel better.

---

doctors	vacations	avoidance	bed
performance	family	sleep	training
driving	prevention	reduction	diet
water	quality	commute	breaks
fitness	technique	surgery	cooking

Staying Healthy at Work

Most of our waking hours are spent at work, which means the working environment can play a big part in our health and well-being.

About 131 million working days were lost through absences due to sickness or injury in 2013. There are many things that workers can do not only to reduce their risk of work-related ill health, but also to use their time at work to boost their health.

Stress   About 15.2 million days were lost last year because of work-related stress, depression and anxiety. While not all stress is work-related, knowing how to deal with a lot of pressure at work is vital. Learn to identify the symptoms of stress. Don't wait for it to make you ill before you do something about it. One of the best ways of dealing with stress is knowing how to prioritise your workload, not doing unsustainably long shifts at work and learning how to say "no" when you're asked to complete more work than you know will be possible to do successfully.

Back Pain   About 30.6 million working days were lost due to work-related back, neck and muscle pain and other musculoskeletal disorders in 2013. The main causes are poor posture or an awkward twisting movement (bending or reaching), or a combination of the two. In most cases, the best treatment is to stay active and, if necessary, use over-the-counter painkillers. You may feel like lying down, but this won't help and could make things worse. The longer you stay immobile, the weaker your back muscles will become and the more they'll hurt in the long term.

RSI   Repetitive strain injury (RSI) is more likely to occur if you spend long periods of work without a break, or if you sit on an uncomfortable chair or at a poorly arranged workstation. Incorrect procedure when using a computer keyboard and mouse, mobile phone or hand-held device can all cause RSI. Modern technology isn't solely responsible. Anyone who uses certain muscles repeatedly can get RSI.

Sitting   If you spend a lot of your time at work sitting at a desk, make sure you're sitting in the right position in relation to your computer. If you're unsure about correct posture, ask your line manager for a workplace assessment. If you work on a computer a lot, it's important to leave the computer periodically. That means for every hour at your keyboard, you should rest for at least five to ten minutes.

Exercise   Many of us spend long hours at work and may have long and tiring journeys to and from work. But getting active at work is easier than you may think. Try and cycle or walk to work, take stairs rather than the lift or use your lunch break as an exercise slot. Do some research and see if there is a gym nearby your offices that you can conveniently visit before work, during lunch break or after work. Working out and losing weight will also benefit your posture and help prevent injury.

Eating   Most people consume over 35 per cent of their daily calorie intake while at work. What we eat and drink affects not just our health, but our efficiency and success too. If we don't eat regular well-balanced meals or drink enough water, we may get headaches, feel sluggish or have difficulty concentrating. We're all guilty sometimes of grabbing some lunch at our desks or even of skipping lunch altogether, but lunch breaks are an ideal time to recharge your batteries by getting some fresh air, taking a walk and getting active.

SECTION 3   *Questions 28 – 40*

Questions 28 – 34

*The text on the following pages has 7 paragraphs (**A – G**).*

Choose the correct heading for each paragraph from the list of headings below.

*Write the correct number, **i - x**, in boxes **28 - 34** on your answer sheet.*

i	Scandal Intervenes
ii	To the Rescue
iii	The Shadow of War
iv	The Beginning of the Project
v	Opposition
vi	Recent Vulnerability and Dealing With It
vii	Rising Costs and Worker Strikes
viii	Building and Safety
ix	An Iconic Symbol
x	Traffic Today

28   Paragraph A

29   Paragraph B

30   Paragraph C

31   Paragraph D

32   Paragraph E

33   Paragraph F

34   Paragraph G

The Golden Gate Bridge

Paragraph A

Nothing identifies a city more than the Golden Gate Bridge does San Francisco. Completed just six months after its neighbour, the San Francisco Oakland Bay Bridge, the Golden Gate Bridge is painted a striking hue known as international orange, a reddish colour that was chosen to compliment the bridge's natural surroundings. Spanning the San Francisco bay the Golden Gate is a suspension bridge, held up by massive steel cables strung between towers. Its central span, at 4,200 feet, remained the longest in the world until 1964. This bridge represents the city it serves probably more than any other bridge in the world and possibly more than any man-made structure.

Paragraph B

The idea of bridging the mile-wide Golden Gate channel was proposed as early as the 1870's, but it was not until the San Francisco Call Bulletin began an editorial campaign in 1916 that the plan received popular backing. Rocky terrain and difficult weather conditions made the task appear impossible and the bridge's detractors publicised this. However, following feasibility studies in 1923, the California legislature passed the Golden Gate Bridge and Highway District Act. The only problem was the funding, which was considerable, as the planning time was following the 1929 stock market crash. Then the Great Depression followed and of course money was hard to come by. It was decided to underwrite a major bond issue of $35,000,000 to fund the bridge. The idea was that tolls paid to cross the bridge would redeem the bond issue, pay the interest and maintenance, and probably make a profit.

Paragraph C

Aesthetes and environmentalists worried the bridge would mar the natural attractiveness of San Francisco's world-famed harbour. A formidable group of civic leaders objected to the financing of the span through the proposed bond measure placed on the ballot for November 1930. Also against the bond measure were the Pacific American Steamship Association and the Ship Owners Association of the Pacific Coast who both charged that the Bridge would be a hazard to navigation and would handicap the shipping industry. A series of other accusations followed: an enemy fleet could demolish the bridge and bottle-up the US fleet. The bridge could not be built. It would not stand. It was vulnerable to earthquakes. The floor of the Golden Gate Strait would not support the load of the bridge. The entire project was a hoax and sham. Only fools would buy bonds of a bridge certain to fall. Taxpayers would suffer and have to continue paying to finance the fiasco.

Paragraph D

Unions, and civic, trade and booster organisations stepped up their campaigns in support of the bond measure. The Redwood Empire Association maintained it would promote tourism in the northern California counties. The California State Automobile Association knew the bridge would encourage auto sales. San Francisco's Chamber of Commerce agreed that the bridge could solve unemployment problems. Voters, despite the financial insecurity that was used as further grounds to oppose the bridge, approved a $35 million construction bond in November 1930.

Paragraph E

Construction began on January 15, 1933 and was completed on May 27, 1937, ahead of schedule and under budget. The engineer overseeing the construction was Joseph Strauss. Strauss had originally wanted a different design for the bridge, but he was advised to accept advice from several consulting project experts. Finally, a suspension bridge was decided upon, due to various new developments in metallurgy. During the construction, Strauss instituted unprecedented protection measures including an early version of the hard hat and a fall net that stretched end-to-end under the bridge. While eleven workers died during the course of the project, nineteen others whose falls were broken by the net became known as the "Half-Way-to-Hell Club."

Paragraph F

In 1989, the Loma Prieta earthquake shook the San Francisco area. Although the Golden Gate Bridge suffered no observed damage from it, since the epicentre was located some 60 miles to the south, the earthquake became a catalyst for an extensive renovation program. After determining that retrofitting the Bridge would be more cost-effective than replacing it, in 1992, the district hired engineering consultants to develop seismic retrofit design criteria. Because of financial constraints, the district proceeded with phasing the construction of the seismic retrofit in a manner that reflected the degrees of structural vulnerabilities. In spite of planning, the costs have spiralled from 300 million dollars to more than 900 million dollars as more work than envisaged became necessary. When the work is completed, an extensive series of tests will be needed to evaluate the effectiveness of the safety measures. Nevertheless, the only true assessment will be the next time a significant earthquake hits the area. The work still goes on today and it is estimated that it will take another two or three years to make the bridge wholly safe from earthquakes.

Paragraph G

The Golden Gate Bridge currently serves as a vital transportation link between the City and County of San Francisco and Marin County to the north. The Bridge is a fixed six-lane roadway, is 1.7 miles long (the main span is 4,200 feet long), and carries about 112,000 vehicles per day. Tolls are assessed electronically in the southbound direction only – heading into San Francisco from Marin County. Pedestrians are allowed, but only on the East Sidewalk and at certain times. Bicycles are allowed, but electric bikes or animals are not.

Questions 35 – 39

Choose **FIVE** letters, **A - I**.

What five of the following reasons were used to oppose the construction of the Golden Gate Bridge?

Write the correct letter, **A - I**, in any order in boxes **35 - 39** on your answer sheet.

A   Unions would oppose the plan.

B   The weather would be too poor at the construction site.

C   The bridge would not look beautiful enough.

D   Tolls for crossing the bridge would not raise enough money to pay back the bonds and their interest.

E   The bridge would potentially threaten the operational capability of the US military forces in San Francisco Bay.

F   The bridge would be bad for tourism in the area of the bridge.

G   The seabed would not be strong enough to hold the bridge's weight.

H   The economic uncertainty of the time would undermine the project.

I   The bridge's construction would destroy the marine ecosystem at the construction site.

Question 40

Choose the correct letter, **A, B, C or D**.

Write the correct letter in box **40** on your answer sheet.

40   What is the writer's purpose in the text in section 3?

A   To criticise construction methods of the Golden Gate Bridge.
B   To highlight the advantages of using the Golden Gate Bridge.
C   To provide an overview of the construction and use of the Golden Gate Bridge.
D   To describe the problems facing the construction of the Golden Gate Bridge.

WRITING

WRITING TASK 1

You should spend about 20 minutes on this task.

You and some friends want to start a weekly dance club and you have found a hall that would be suitable to hold your meetings.

Write a letter to the owner of the hall. In your letter,

- **explain your and your friends' project**
- **ask if it is possible to rent the hall and under what terms**
- **state what day and what times you would like to use the hall**

You should write at least 150 words.

*You do **NOT** need to write any addresses. Begin your letter as follows:*

Dear Sir / Madam,

WRITING TASK 2

You should spend about 40 minutes on this task.

Write about the following topic:

Some people believe that the problem of illegal drugs can be solved by just legalising all drugs.

To what extent do you agree or disagree with this?

Give reasons for your answer and include any relevant examples from your knowledge or experience.

You should write at least 250 words.

SPEAKING

PART 1

- Describe one of your childhood friends.
- Did you have a lot of friends when you were young?
- Do you stay in touch with any of your childhood friends?

Topic 1   Dancing

- Do you like dancing? (Why/Why not?)
- Why do you think people dance?
- What kinds of dancing can be seen in your country?
- Do you think it's important that countries' traditional dances are preserved? (Why/Why not?)

Topic 2   Dentists

- How do you feel about visits to the dentist?
- Why do you think some people are scared of visits to the dentist?
- What are dentists like in your country?
- How have equipment and anaesthetics changed what dentistry can do?

PART 2

Describe a memorable job that you once had.
You should say:
        where this job was
        when you did this job
        what you did in this job
and briefly explain why this job was so memorable.

PART 3

Topic 1   Poverty

- What is poverty?
- What kinds of poverty exist in your country?
- What kinds of things can governments do to tackle poverty?
- How do you think poverty will change over the next 50 years?

Topic 2   Wealth

- Do you think wealth can lead to happiness?
- Is there a severe wealth gap in your country?
- Do you think it's fair that so much of the world's wealth is shared by so few people?
- Do you think the wealthy should be taxed more?

PRACTICE TEST 13

LISTENING

 Download audio recordings for the test here:
https://www.ielts-blog.com/ielts-practice-tests-downloads/

PART 1   Questions 1 – 10

Questions 1 – 5

Complete Happies Nursery's new child enrolment form below.

*Write **NO MORE THAN THREE WORDS AND/OR A NUMBER** from the listening for each answer.*

Happies Nursery
New Child Enrolment Form

Parents' Names -	Father:	Luke Beckett	
	Mother:	**(1)** _____ Beckett	*Gloria*
Address:		**(2)** _____ Castle Crescent	*40*
		Backley	
Postcode:		BA3 7TR	
Telephone Numbers:			
Home	Father:	01538 853 285	
	Mother:	Same as father's	
Mobile	Father:	07770 728 473	
	Mother:	07743 812 **(3)** *451*	
Work	Father:	01538 926 477	
	Mother:	01538 596 821	
Fees will be paid by:		**(4)** *Bank transfer*	
Allergies:		**(5)** *Cats*	

Questions 6 – 10

Complete Luke's notes for his wife below.

Write **NO MORE THAN TWO WORDS AND/OR A NUMBER** from the listening for each answer.

Happies Nursery – Notes

* Activities start at (**6**) _8:30_ a.m. - parents can drop their children off after 6.30 a.m.
* From 6.30 a.m., there's a team of carers for supervision, cleaning and changing.
* All we need to bring are a sweater and some extra (**7**) _____ in a marked bag.
  changes of clothing
* Happies will call if Gertrude is sick - we'll have to pick her up if this happens.
* Happies is 1 mile from the County Hospital and there's always a (**8**) _____ on the premises for health supervision.   _Nurse_

* Activities end at 4.00 p.m. (we can pick Gertrude up earlier if we want).
* Children are supervised until 6.30 p.m.
* We mustn't come after 6.30 p.m. and we should call the number in the (**9**) _____ if we're delayed.   _Information pack_

* Happies runs a new service - supervision during the (**10**) _____. It could be useful for us sometimes.   _weekends_

PART 2   *Questions 11 – 20*

Questions 11 – 15

Complete the sentences below.

*Write **NO MORE THAN TWO WORDS AND/OR A NUMBER** from the listening for each answer.*

11   Green Trees can accommodate a maximum of _____ [60] people.

12   Green Trees does not cater for caring for _____. [Married couples]

13   If residents communicate with Green Trees, they can arrange _____ to be prepared. [special diets]

14   Green Trees tries to combine care and nursing with opportunities for residents to remain as _____ as possible. [independent]

15   Green Trees' fees can be found in their leaflets or on the _____. [website]

Questions 16 – 20

Complete the table below.

Write **NO MORE THAN TWO WORDS AND/OR A NUMBER** *from the listening for each answer.*

Green Trees Old Age Centre		
What	**When**	**Notes**
Games Room Activities	Twice weekly	* Cards, bingo etc. * A (**16**) *guest* _____ is permitted to be invited - residents can meet new people
Puzzle Sessions	Regular	* Crosswords, sudoku etc.
Telling Life Stories	Not mentioned	* Sometimes not easy, but brings back lost memories * Can be recorded or written down * Good for the younger generation
All these above activities promote good condition in the (**17**) _____ and lead to all sorts of other benefits. *Brain fitness*		
Trips Away	Regular	* Trips to various places, including shows, markets and places of interest * Only (**18**) *1 DAY* _____ trips arranged to prevent resident fatigue * Residents' families can take residents away for overnight trips - inform Green Trees when this happens
Gardening	Suitable weather *Isolation* *Special tools*	* Very fulfilling * Caring for plants helps combat sense of (**19**) _____ and makes residents feel in control * Very popular activity * Can be dangerous, but training and (**20**) _____ are provided * Supervised by the two gardeners

PART 3   Questions 21 – 30

Questions 21 – 25

Choose the correct letter A, B, or C.

21   Lily's engineering placement will be working

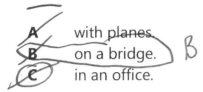

   A   with planes.
   B   on a bridge.
   C   in an office.

22   Ross' engineering placement will be

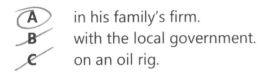

   A   in his family's firm.
   B   with the local government.
   C   on an oil rig.

23   Derek was refused an engineering placement in the Antarctic, because

   A   of the extreme cold.
   B   his father had to go to hospital.
   C   of a previous health problem.

24   Tanya's engineering placement will involve working with her

   A   tutor's contacts.
   B   cousin.
   C   boyfriend.

25   The students must send their engineering placement notifications to their department

   A   verbally.
   B   by email.
   C   by hand.

Questions 26 – 28

Complete the diagram below on the gas drilling station where Tanya will do her engineering placement.

Write **NO MORE THAN TWO WORDS** from the listening for each answer.

Gas Drilling Station

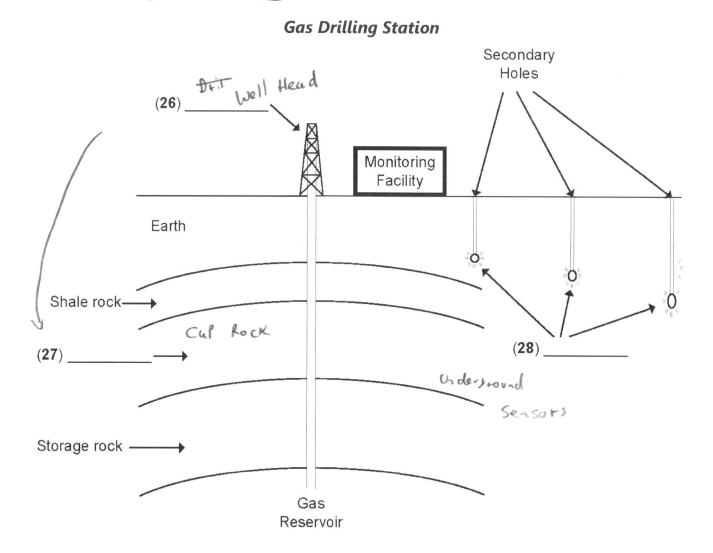

Questions 29 and 30

Answer the questions below. Write **NO MORE THAN TWO WORDS AND/OR A NUMBER** from the listening for each answer.

29   How will Tanya's team in the desert be in contact with their head office?

                eMail

30   How long will Tanya spend in the desert at any one time?

           4 weeks   Page 56

PART 4   *Questions 31 – 40*

Questions 31 – 37

Complete the summary below on the lecture on hypnosis, hypnotism and hypnotherapy.

Write NO MORE THAN TWO WORDS from the listening for each answer.

Hypnosis, Hypnotism and Hypnotherapy

Definitions

Hypnosis - a different psychological state of consciousness with increased potential for (**31**) _____.   Influence

Hypnotism - the study of hypnosis or the study of using suggestion during hypnosis.

Hypnotherapy - a therapy conducted mainly during hypnosis.

Discussion

Hypnosis creates such relaxation that certain suggestions may be made to the (**32**) _____,   *Mind* bypassing the awake and logical part of the brain, so that therapy is possible. The hypnotic trance allows increased (**33**) _____ to create beneficial changes. Usually the hypnotic trance is medium, which slows certain body functions, while the brain creates alpha waves. This condition is different to normal states of consciousness, as alpha waves signify a special (**34**) _____ *trance*

Not yet fully understood, a favoured theory is that hypnosis influences how people pay attention, which happens in the brain stem's ascending reticular formation. This area receives stimuli from the (**35**) _____ and passes on messages to the rest of the brain. Hypnosis may inhibit this area, creating great calm.   *Brain stem*

Hypnotherapy works by exploring the subconscious, where people have unrealised problems, self images, strengths and knowledge. Using hypnotherapy can exploit people's unknown (**36**) _____ and help solve problems. Many techniques are used by the hypnotherapist in the hypnotic trance. Some hypnotherapy requires little change in a patient, but more complicated behaviours require deeper therapy and psychological (**37**) _____ *state*.   *Subconscious*

Questions 38 - 40

*Choose **THREE** letters, **A - G**.*

According to the listening, why has hypnotherapy been criticised?

A   Because any practitioners are not properly qualified.

B   Because not enough research has been done to back up the results.

C   Because the relationship between hypnotherapy and improved patient results is not easy to prove.

D   Because current tests do not use a big enough sample of the population.

E   Because some tests have shown that hypnotherapy has only had an effect because the patients thought it would.

F   Because patients give positive responses when questioned in tests because they think they ought to.

G   Because of ignorance of hypnotherapy in the critics.

little   knowledge

READING

SECTION 1   *Questions 1 – 14*

Questions 1 – 8

*There are 8 advertisements **A – H** on the next page.*

*Answer the questions below by writing the letters of the appropriate advertisements in boxes **1 – 8** on your answer sheet. Some letters may be used more than once.*

1   However long it takes, this worker has a minimum amount that must be paid if he or she comes to a job.

2   This worker can supply recommendations from previous customers.

3   This worker wants to be contacted by email.

4   This worker wants to be paid by card.

5   This worker can supervise children in the mornings.

6   This worker needs to be provided with transport to get home at certain times.

7   This worker will wash your clothes.

8   This worker has a website that people can use to order the service.

A   Hello. My name's John and I am an odd job man. I can do any repair or maintenance work around the house, though I specialise in working with wood. Making wood furniture made to measure is something I'm particularly well known for. Call me on 01564 398 877 if you need something done!

B   Experienced gardener available to work mornings in this area. I have lots of experience with creating and maintaining beautiful lawns and I have plenty of experience with landscaping and planting and nurturing flowers. I can also plan and set up kitchen gardens or I can just come in and give you advice about your garden. References available on request. Call 07454 893 212.

C   Babysitter for you! Hi. I'm Sally and I'm a student at the local university. I offer babysitting services on any evening of the week. I am available from 6 p.m. every weekday and from 4 p.m. at weekends. I charge $10 an hour and I ask for a taxi to take me home if I stay at your home after 11 p.m. Overnight stays are possible with older children. If you want to have a chat about what I can do, contact me at sallv@online.com.au.

D   Home Cleaning. I am an efficient cleaner in your area with years of experience who can work mornings only (8 a.m. – 12 noon - weekdays and weekends). I can do all types of housework, and I can also handle your laundry, ironing, washing up or childcare.
Call my mobile: 07864 382 855.

E   Mike the Electrician. If you have any issues with the electrics in your house, then I'm the man to call. I can do anything from a total rewire of your home to changing a bulb. Many houses today have wildly out-of-date wiring, so call me to come and have a look for free and I'll provide you with an analysis of your requirements and a quotation 07232 767434 ($60 call-out charge).

F   Home Shopping. For people who can't get out and about, I will come to your house or receive a phone call for your shopping needs and then I'll bring it all back to your house and put it into the right place. I charge an hourly rate of $10 with pro rata for time between the hours.
Call Alex on 07821 441 448.

G   Hayley's Car Servicing. My garage and team of mechanics will give your car a careful check over and get it back to you on the same day (providing we get it before midday). We can also deal with any "yellow sticker" problems right away. Car valeting service available as well.
Phone: 01564 902 993.

H   Home Cooking. For those people who might find it hard to cook a meal at home (or for those who just don't have time), I provide a cooking and meal delivery service. All you need to do is to place an order from our menu list before 7 p.m. the previous night and we'll bring it to your house. Call or use our website to place your orders. All payments to be done by credit or debit card at the time of ordering. Make sure to give us details of any allergies that you might suffer from. www.foodforyou.com.au / 01564 555 444.

Questions 9 – 14

Answer the questions below.

Write **NO MORE THAN THREE WORDS** from the text for each answer.

Write your answers in boxes **9 - 14** on your answer sheet.

9   Who should people speak to if they wish to change the sitting they will attend for dinner?

10   What must people give to have the use of a sun lounger on the beach?

11   Who should people ask to see if they're sick in the hotel?

12   Who are the only people who can use the hotel swimming pool?

13   How will drinks be served at the hotel swimming pool?

14   Where will people find information about the evening shows and fun at the hotel?

Hotel Amenities

Welcome to the Bayside Hotel. This paper will explain to you some of the basics you'll need to know about during your stay with us.

Food

Breakfast is buffet style and served every morning in the Seaview restaurant, found on the 2nd floor. Breakfast is served every day from 6 a.m. until 10 a.m. If you're up earlier and in a hurry for a plane or a train, we will have "Breakfast on the Go" available at the reception. Pick up some coffee or tea, and some filled rolls or fruit (available from 4 a.m. until 7a.m.).

For those people who have lunch in their package or want to order lunch, it too is buffet style and available in the Seaview restaurant from 12 noon until 3 p.m.

Dinner is served at two sittings, the first is from 5.30 p.m. until 7.30 p.m. and the second is from 7.45 p.m. until 10 p.m. Ask the head waiter which sitting you have been allocated. She can change this if space is available. Again, dinner is buffet style and served in the Seaview restaurant. If you'd like to order à la carte, you may go to the top floor Oyster Restaurant. Eating at this restaurant is not included in package prices.

The Beach

Residents only may use our private beach at any time, though the lifeguards are on duty only from 9 a.m. until 7 p.m. We discourage swimming outside these hours, as there will be no supervision. All sun loungers and tables on the beach are free of charge for our residents, but a small deposit is required. Food and drinks may be ordered at the snack bar in the pool area and these can be brought to your place on the beach. If you have any minor accident on the beach, such as a minor cut, speak to our lifeguards, who are all first aid trained. For anything more serious or problems in the hotel, there is the nurse on duty 24/7 in the hotel. Ask at reception if you need him/her.

The Pool Area

The main hotel swimming pool area is also solely accessible by hotel residents. Sun loungers and tables are free of charge, but they may not be 'reserved' unattended for long periods of time. The pool is open for swimming 24-hours a day, but, like the beach, a lifeguard is only on duty from 9 a.m. until 7 p.m. People may order food and drinks at the snack bar. The food can be eaten on the tables at the snack bar or on the sun loungers and tables. Please note that all drinks will be supplied in plastic receptacles, as glass can be a potential danger by the pool. The pool is not suitable for young children. A paddling pool is available for young children (accompanied by an adult) to the west of the main pool.

Entertainment

Every evening from 7 p.m., we have entertainment around the pool. This will vary from music recitals and singing to quiz and games nights. Check the entertainment board for the weekly plan.

For any further information about any of the above, please speak to one of our receptionists, who will be happy to deal with your questions.

SECTION 2   *Questions 15 – 27*

Questions 15 – 21

Complete the notes below.

Write **NO MORE THAN TWO WORDS** *for each answer.*

Write your answers in boxes **15 - 21** *on your answer sheet.*

Advice on How to Resign

* It's best to resign in writing and give the (**15**) _____ that is stated in your contract, although talking informally with your boss first is a nice courtesy.

* You don't need to give a reason.

* You're entitled to the usual (**16**) _____ and other work conditions until you leave.

* It's best to write a resignation letter with the necessary formalities. Show that you are grateful and that you want a smooth handover. Maybe mention any important unfinished (**17**) _____ related to your post.

* You might be offered a (**18**) _____ with better pay/promotion/benefits. Consider this carefully before accepting or rejecting it.

* Don't resign when angry – the employers might still accept the resignation if you change your mind.

* You might be asked to leave immediately in return for a paid sum (**19**) _____, or work somewhere else.

* A restrictive covenant might prevent you joining a competitor or dealing with your old customers – this is legally enforceable.

* Leave on good terms in case you require a (**20**) _____. You may also work with the same people again.

* As some colleagues may have to cover your old (**21**) _____, don't expect everyone to be happy that you are leaving.

Advice on How to Resign

Employees in this country terminate their contract by resigning. Employees should make it clear that they are formally resigning and it would be best to do this in writing giving the correct amount of notice. It might be good to have an informal conversation with your boss before out of politeness, as this can cause good will, but you are not obliged to provide a reason for your resignation. You must tell your employer 1 week in advance if you want to leave your job if you've worked for them for 1 month or more, unless it says differently in your contract. You're usually due the normal pay and things like sick leave before you leave. The time before you leave usually runs from the start of the day after you gave in your resignation.

If you write a resignation letter (and you should), there are certain things you should include. Your letter should include the position you're resigning from and the date you intend to leave. Although not essential, you might want to thank your employer for the opportunities you've been given and offer your willingness to ensure a smooth handover. Although you don't need to give details at this point, it might be a good idea to let your company know if there are any outstanding issues you're dealing with that might be affected by your leaving.

If you're a good employee and you've done a good job, the chances are your boss won't want to see you go. The most likely way an employer will try and make you stay is by proposing a pay rise either equal to or above what you've been offered in your new job and/or by suggesting promotion and/or added benefits. Make sure you understand the counter offer and avoid making a knee jerk decision. While the promise of promotion, increased responsibility and extra money may sound tempting, will it really make you want to stay for the next few years? Think carefully about what's been suggested, but don't forget that you'll be working in the same organisation, with the same people and probably under the same boss. Don't be persuaded into staying simply because you're scared of change. It can be tempting to accept because you're comfortable where you are.

If you resign in the 'heat of the moment' (e.g. during an argument) and you change your mind, you should tell your employer immediately. They can choose if they want to accept your resignation or not.

Once you resign, your employer can ask you to leave immediately. In this case they'll probably offer you a one-off payment in lieu, instead of allowing you to work out your time. This amount can be negotiated with your employer. You can also be made to work from home (or another location) until you leave.

Your contract may include a restrictive covenant, which is a period of time that your employer wants to stop you from working for a competitor, or having contact with customers, once you've left the company. You can be taken to court if you break a restrictive covenant.

Try and leave your job on a suitable footing with people. Firstly, any new employer may want a reference from your old employer. While your old employer is not allowed to say bad things about you, they can refuse to issue a reference, which is a very bad sign for a new employer. Secondly, you may find that, in the future, you will work with some of your ex-colleagues and it would be bad to have poor relationships still existing.

Don't expect everyone to be glad about your leaving. Some people might take it personally and it might mean that some of your co-workers have to take on the responsibilities that you are leaving.

Questions 22 – 27

Complete each sentence with the correct ending (**A - I**) below.

Write the correct letter (**A - I**) in boxes **22 - 27** on your answer sheet.

22   The new punctuality policy will help managers to

23   A lack of punctuality can often force co-workers to

24   Seeing co-workers arriving late without action being taken can lead to

25   The meeting next week will lead to

26   The drafts of the new punctuality will

27   Signing the punctuality policy will help to

A   lead to the punctuality policy being implemented immediately.

B   be accountable for their own and others' work.

C   be shown to staff before the policy is definitively issued.

D   be responsible for their own actions.

E   be forced to find a job elsewhere.

F   deal with this sometimes emotive situation.

G   all workers being involved in the punctuality policy's creation.

H   other workers leaving early.

I   punctual co-workers feeling demoralised.

Our New Punctuality Policy

As the company management has recently noticed a number of employees arriving late to work, the company has decided to implement a punctuality policy. The policy will be created in liaison with all our employees, so that everyone knows where they stand and that they will be treated fairly.

Punctuality is always a difficult thing for managers to enforce, as there are often reasons for lateness. No supervisor likes to be heavy-handed and antagonise people. On the other hand, other employees may feel frustrated by colleagues who routinely show up late. If the issue isn't addressed by management, a sense of preferential treatment may occur because a colleague is getting away with unprofessional behaviour. The policy will therefore help support the supervisors as well as make things clear for all employees.

Lateness affects employee productivity. The late employee cannot complete tasks, is not there to take part in teams and will need to be covered by colleagues, which stops the colleagues from fulfilling their own responsibilities. This can be very demotivating for the late workers' colleagues.

Next week at 10 a.m., we will be holding a mandatory meeting for all staff, where the draft policy will be discussed. All employees will be allowed to ask questions and make their points of view known. Notes will be taken of the meeting and shared by email, so that everyone can see how all viewpoints will be taken note of. If any employee cannot make this meeting due to work responsibilities, they should communicate with their line manager so that they have the chance to ask questions and make their opinions known.

Our policy will define "punctual" for all our employees. This should include employees being at the work stations and ready to work no later than the shift starting time. The policy should also include the consequences for showing up late or not being prepared to work. This may range from light punishment such as a verbal warning to severe punishment such as termination. A termination would typically occur after several incidents of being late, which should be clearly defined in the policy. This allows all employees to know exactly what will happen and when if they continue showing up late.

After next week's meeting, a draft punctuality policy will be drawn up by the Human Resources Department. The draft will be first reviewed by senior management, who will recommend changes as they see fit. When the next draft is ready, the policy will be shared with all employees and everyone will be given the chance to give feedback and voice concerns. After all the feedback has been collected and assessed, the final policy will be published.

When the policy is ready, all employees will be asked to add their signature to it to show they have read and understood everything in it. It's important to highlight that after this the policy will be put into action straight away, and management will be sure to follow through with the consequences, so that the employees who are abusing the current system don't try to get away with continued tardiness.

Any employee with a disability will have no reason to worry, as the policy will reflect the extra difficulties that these employees face. For example, if an employee relies on public transportation or is otherwise unable to arrive to work at a specified time due to his/her disability, flexibility in the punctuality policy is a possible accommodation.

SECTION 3   *Questions 28 – 40*

*Read the following passage and answer Questions **28 – 40**.*

The Australian Dingo Fence

Australia is a land with many famous landmarks and is blessed with different magnificent landscapes from desert to mountains. Perhaps Australia's most iconic division is a basic two-metre-high fence. This fence may be basic in its construction, but it certainly is not by length at 5614 kilometers. The world's longest fence, known as the Dingo Fence or Dog Fence, has split Australia in two for the past one hundred and thirty years.

The dingo, the wild dog of the Australian continent and the largest carnivorous mammal in the country, has been seen as a nuisance animal on agricultural lands dating back to the beginning of European settlement in the region, predating the valuable sheep flocks that cover much of southeastern Australia. The dingo's origin is uncertain, though scientists now believe that it is related to the Asian and Middle Eastern wolf that probably arrived in Australia between 3,500 and 4,000 years ago, transported by Asian seafarers.

The first merino sheep flocks were brought to Australia in the 1800's. When grazing began in the northern plains of South Australia in about 1860, the first 30 years were relatively free of dingoes. However, dingo populations multiplied and evidence has shown that they began to thrive on the newly imported European rabbits that were running in feral plagues at the same time.

By the early 1900's, dingo attacks had made it impossible to successfully establish a sheep industry. Bounties have been placed on the heads of dingoes in southeastern Australia since as early as 1852. While bounties were placed on numerous types of animals, the bounties given for dingoes were generally the highest and often twice as much was given for a dingo than for other pests, such as foxes, hares, and wallabies. The most effective method of preventing dingoes from killing sheep in southeastern Australia, however, was to stop them from entering it in the first place. Sheep graziers began building fences around their properties to protect their flocks from the predatory dingo. As time went on, neighbouring livestock properties grouped together to become enclosed within vermin-proof fences. Rapidly expanding fenced properties joined up to become what were termed vermin-proof districts. At the peak of these vermin-proof districts, there were over 30,000 miles of these fences. In 1946, a single-line dog fence was established in South Australia to align with the most northern boundaries of the properties contained within the vermin proof districts. It now extends from the Great Australian Bight eastward across South Australia, through New South Wales, to finish near the Pacific coast. Over time, the length of the fence has also been reduced within Queensland for cost reasons and control over the dingo population is often done via less expensive poisoning, specifically via bait laced with sodium monofluoroacetate.

While dingoes remain common in the northern half of Australia, they are almost non-existent in most places on the south side of the fence, except for the strip of land between the Pacific Coast and the Great Dividing Range, where no fencing exists. Despite maintenance and patrol, holes have developed in the fence over the years, particularly in South Australia, and dingo offspring have been passing through them and predating on sheep on the other side, greatly affecting the ability of farmers to stay afloat. Feral camels are also smashing through sections of the fence in search of water and recommendations to reinforce and electrify more portions of the fence have been made to deal with this.

The Dog Fence Board is the governing body set up to administer and manage the Dog Fence and ensure that it is regularly patrolled and maintained. The Dog Fence Act 1946 levied a rate on grazing properties located inside the fence to fund wages for maintenance and patrol workers. Since 1947, the fence within South Australia has been continuously maintained, re-aligned and upgraded. New fencing technology has also been incorporated and dog-proof grids at road crossings and solar-powered electrified sections have been introduced.

The type of fence that is mostly used today is the sloping dog fence. Every section of the fence is just over a metre high and has six wires, consecutively electrically charged and earthed, that go between timber posts down from the top until around 30 centimetres from the bottom. The lower wires then angle out to the ground at approximately a 30-degree angle with four more wires, again consecutively electrically charged and earthed. These angled bottom wires are more narrowly spaced, as this is where pressure from dingoes is greatest. The sloping wire arrangement may also slow the approach of animals to the fence.

This fence is cheaper to construct and maintain compared to the composite dog fence, which goes under the ground. The sloping dog fence is recommended for most locations, except in situations where the soil is susceptible to erosion, as this may result in the formation of gaps below the fence. The positioning of electric wires close to the ground is also likely to result in the death of other animals and, as a result, in places where lots of other species are in danger, this design is avoided. The fence's low electric wires are also likely to be problematic in environments with considerable ground vegetation, which will cause electrical shorts and leakage.

Questions 28 – 32

Do the following statements agree with the information given in the text?

*In boxes **28 – 32** on your answer sheet write:*

TRUE	*if the statement agrees with the information*
FALSE	*if the statement contradicts the information*
NOT GIVEN	*if there is no information on this*

28   No one is really sure where the dingo originally comes from.

29   Studies into dingo populations have shown that they have different species in different parts of Australia.

30   The introduction of other non-native animal species boosted dingo numbers.

31   People could earn more money killing dingoes than they could by killing other nuisance species.

32   Generally, farms created individual solutions to the dingo problem

Questions 33 – 37

*Choose the correct letter **A, B, C or D**.*

*Write the correct letter in boxes **33 - 37** on your answer sheet.*

33   Killing dingoes in Queensland with poison is done because

     A   animal rights activists opposed the electrocution of the dingoes.
     B   too many other species were killed by the dingo fence.
     C   it's cheaper than building and maintaining the dingo fence.
     D   the weather degraded the dingo fence too quickly.

34   Electrifying more sections of the dingo fence

     A   is opposed by most farmers because of the costs.
     B   will lead to more complex maintenance requirements.
     C   will be subsidised by the Australian government.
     D   will prevent damage to the fence by other animals.

35   Farms protected by the dingo fence today

     A   are responsible for the maintenance of their part of the fence.
     B   have to supply the electricity for the electrified sections.
     C   have to pay a charge for the protection.
     D   receive financial support for any livestock killed by dingoes breaking through the fence.

36   The sloping dog fence is not suitable for

     A   areas where feral camels are common.
     B   areas where the ground can wear away and leave holes.
     C   areas that need a lot of maintenance.
     D   areas that are composed largely of rock.

37   The wires at the bottom of the sloping dog fence

     A   are susceptible to developing faults.
     B   are difficult to maintain.
     C   carry a lower charge.
     D   prevent vegetation from growing into the fence.

Questions 38 – 40

Label the diagram below.

Write **NO MORE THAN THREE WORDS AND/OR A NUMBER** *from the text for each answer.*

Write your answers in boxes **38 - 40** *on your answer sheet.*

A Section of a Sloping Dog Fence

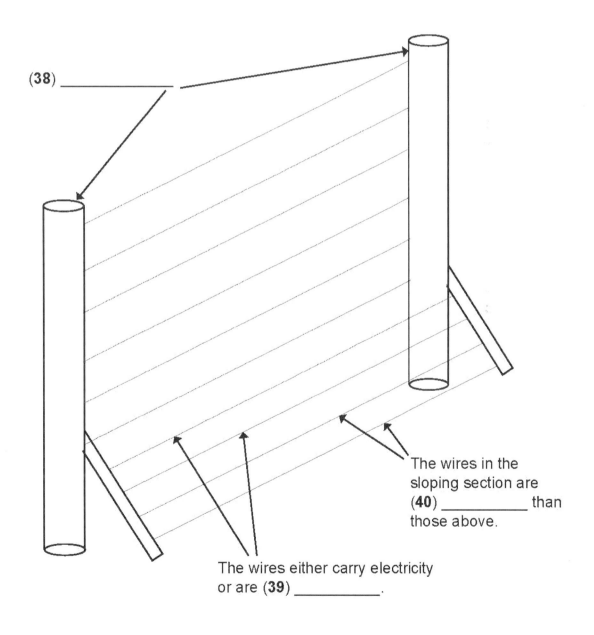

(38) _____

The wires in the sloping section are (40) _____ than those above.

The wires either carry electricity or are (39) _____.

WRITING

WRITING TASK 1

You should spend about 20 minutes on this task.

A friend is expecting you to stay with him in two weeks' time, but unfortunately you forgot that you have a business trip at the same time.

Write a letter to your friend. In your letter,

- **apologise and say that you cannot come to visit**
- **explain why you will not be able to visit**
- **suggest another time that you could visit**

You should write at least 150 words.

*You do **NOT** need to write any addresses. Begin your letter as follows:*

Dear Tom,

WRITING TASK 2

You should spend about 40 minutes on this task.

Write about the following topic:

Providing a national system in a country where the unemployed receive a regular payment only encourages people not to seek work and puts an unreasonable strain on a country's financial resources.

Discuss this statement and give your opinion.

Give reasons for your answer and include any relevant examples from your knowledge or experience.

You should write at least 250 words.

SPEAKING

PART 1

- Describe the street where you grew up when you were young.
- Was there a good community spirit where you grew up?
- What kinds of things do you remember about your neighbours from where you grew up?

Topic 1　　Shopping
- Who does the grocery shopping in your household?
- Do you prefer a supermarket or visiting markets and smaller shops? (Why?)
- Do you like to shop online? (Why/Why not?)
- What are your feelings about people who are addicted to shopping?

Topic 2　　Immigration
- Does your country experience much immigration and emigration? (Why/Why not?)
- How is immigration helpful to a country?
- What things should immigrants know before they move to another country?
- Do you think countries should drop all restrictions on immigration? (Why/Why not?)

PART 2

Describe a well-known building in your country that you like.
You should say:
　　　where this building is
　　　what the function of the building is
　　　what people think about the building
and explain why you like this building.

PART 3

Topic 1　　Architecture
- What do you think about your country's old and modern styles of architecture?
- What do you feel about the increase of people living in apartment blocks?
- What are some of the factors that affect architectural decisions?
- How do you think your country's architecture will change over the next 50 years?

Topic 2　　Preserving Old Buildings
- What are the most significant old buildings and monuments in your country?
- Do you prefer old buildings or new buildings? (Why?)
- How important is it to preserve national monuments and famous buildings?
- Do you think people should be able to visit monuments and famous buildings for free or should they pay? (Why?)

PRACTICE TEST 14

LISTENING

 Download audio recordings for the test here:
https://www.ielts-blog.com/ielts-practice-tests-downloads/

PART 1   *Questions 1 – 10*

Questions 1 – 6

Complete Mrs. Davis' notes below.

Write **NO MORE THAN THREE WORDS AND/OR A NUMBER** *from the listening for each answer.*

Dominic's Summer Sports Camp

The sports coaching is done by sports science students, who are supervised by
(**1**) _____ with more experience. All staff have an enhanced police check and company
training. They are also trained in (**2**) _____ and there's a hospital nearby.

Dominic will need warm clothing and changes of clothing in case of bad weather. If weather
is bad, everyone will move into the (**3**) _____ of Wentmount School.

Sessions   Morning, afternoon or both. Dominic can do both and make some new
                friends.

Food   Give Dominic a packed lunch or he can join the group lunches.
                Group Lunches - Basic starter; hot main course; (**4**) _____ to finish with.

Dominic will need his sports equipment that he wants to bring and some (**5**) _____ for
between meals.

Timings   Morning Session   9.30 a.m. - 12.00 midday
                Afternoon Session 1.30 p.m. - (**6**) _____ p.m.

Children must be picked up by 5 p.m.

Questions 7 – 10

*Choose the correct letter **A, B, or C**.*

7   Dominic's favourite sport is

    A   cricket.
    B   swimming.
    C   football.

8   Mrs. Davis says that the instructors should know that

    A   Dominic's legs are weak.
    B   Dominic will have to go to hospital at the start of the summer.
    C   Dominic broke his arm during the winter.

9   The first week of the camp, Dominic will

    A   be picked up by his mother.
    B   go home by bus.
    C   walk home with friends.

10   To keep Dominic's reserved place on the sports camp, Mrs. Davis has to return the form

    A   within two weeks.
    B   the next day.
    C   within a week.

PART 2   *Questions 11 – 20*

Questions 11 – 15

*Match the situation given (questions **11 - 15**) with the advice given in the listening by Police Constable Dawson (**A - I**).*

*Write the correct letter (**A - I**) next to questions 11 - 15.*

11   Your bicycle has been stolen.   _____

12   You are worried that someone is following you.   _____

13   You've bought a car.   _____

14   Your house is broken into, but your bank cards are not taken.   _____

15   You need to throw away some documents that have sensitive information.   _____

A	Cancel your bank cards.
B	Establish a security routine.
C	Find a secure storage place for your bank cards.
D	Go to a nearby shop and explain what has happened.
E	Make sure a photo and description goes to the police.
F	Hide behind a nearby car.
G	Burn them.
H	Buy a paper shredder.
I	Search the nearby area.

Questions 16 – 20

Complete the sentences below.

Write **NO MORE THAN TWO WORDS** *from the listening for each answer.*

16   _____ is what allows cell phone thieves to succeed.

17   Pickpockets like stealing in busy _____, so be extra aware in these places.

18   People leaving subway stations often have their cell phones stolen when they look to see if they have a _____.

19   People should consult their _____ to find out how to switch on the security features available on their cell phones.

20   If your cell phone is stolen, the police have to know more than its _____ and colour if they are to get it back to you.

PART 3   Questions 21 – 30

Questions 21 – 25

Complete the summary below on the Kenyan flower industry.

*Write **NO MORE THAN TWO WORDS** from the listening for each answer.*

The Kenyan Flower Industry

The Kenyan flower industry is Kenya's largest after (**21**) _____ and tea and has increased by 31% over the last 5 years. Originally started to contribute to British East Africa's (**22**) _____, it continued to flourish after independence due to its geographical position and variety of climate conditions.

Economic advantages, such as beneficial (**23**) _____ have kept costs low and good logistics have been set up to service world flower markets. Labour and energy costs are also low and there is no (**24**) _____ on European exports from Kenya.

Floriculture is Kenya's 2nd highest foreign exchange earner and it generates plenty of (**25**) _____ for Kenya's public economy - 50,000 to 70,000 people are employed directly and 1½ million people indirectly.

Questions 26 – 30

Complete the table below on problems and criticisms of the Kenyan flower industry.

Write **NO MORE THAN TWO WORDS** from the listening for each answer.

Problems and Criticisms	
Workforce Disputes	* Not wholly resolved yet
High Oil Prices	* Increased (**26**) _____ costs
Heavy Rains + Extended Drought	* Affected the crop size
Competition	* Mostly from countries on or near the equator * Biggest competitors - The Netherlands, Colombia, Ecuador and Ethiopia * Competition getting fiercer due to the numbers of roses produced and better (**27**) _____ from the competition.
Sustainability	* Wages are often too low - workers have a problem with poor disposable income * Trade unions are discouraged
Water Usage	* 1 rose's water footprint is 7 - 13 litres * There has been a very large water export within the flowers out of the country * Lakes have declined in level and (**28**) _____
Pollution	* In local lakes * Large producers initially blamed, but it's now proved that small holders are also to blame * The nutrient load in lakes is too high * Attempts at improvement by increasing the price of (**29**) _____ and other regulatory measures - political and tribal issues have resisted these attempted efforts
Outdated Farm Methods	* Improving situation * More organic ways of (**30**) _____ are being used * More water recycling and waste disposal systems in participating farms have led to long-term costs savings

PART 4   *Questions 31 – 40*

Questions 31 – 37

Complete the flow chart that summarises the cotton growing process.

*Write **NO MORE THAN TWO WORDS** from the listening for each answer.*

Growing Cotton

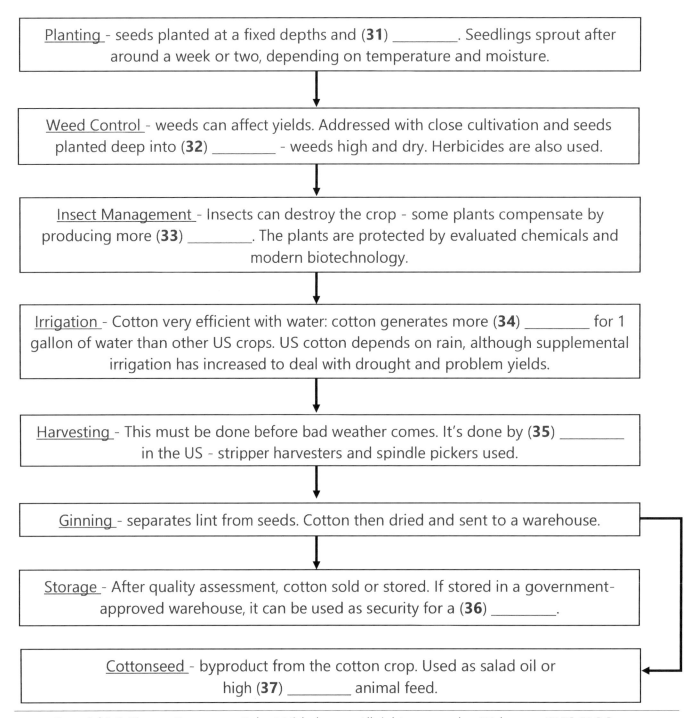

Planting - seeds planted at a fixed depths and (**31**) _____. Seedlings sprout after around a week or two, depending on temperature and moisture.

Weed Control - weeds can affect yields. Addressed with close cultivation and seeds planted deep into (**32**) _____ - weeds high and dry. Herbicides are also used.

Insect Management - Insects can destroy the crop - some plants compensate by producing more (**33**) _____. The plants are protected by evaluated chemicals and modern biotechnology.

Irrigation - Cotton very efficient with water: cotton generates more (**34**) _____ for 1 gallon of water than other US crops. US cotton depends on rain, although supplemental irrigation has increased to deal with drought and problem yields.

Harvesting - This must be done before bad weather comes. It's done by (**35**) _____ in the US - stripper harvesters and spindle pickers used.

Ginning - separates lint from seeds. Cotton then dried and sent to a warehouse.

Storage - After quality assessment, cotton sold or stored. If stored in a government-approved warehouse, it can be used as security for a (**36**) _____.

Cottonseed - byproduct from the cotton crop. Used as salad oil or high (**37**) _____ animal feed.

Questions 38 – 40

Complete the diagram below of the three nozzle positions for crop-spraying cotton.

Write **NO MORE THAN THREE WORDS** from the listening for each answer.

Three Nozzle Positions for Crop-spraying Cotton

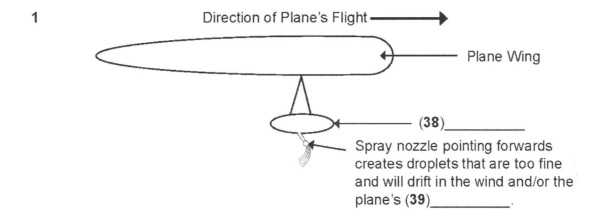

1

Direction of Plane's Flight ➞

Plane Wing

(38)_____

Spray nozzle pointing forwards creates droplets that are too fine and will drift in the wind and/or the plane's (39)_____.

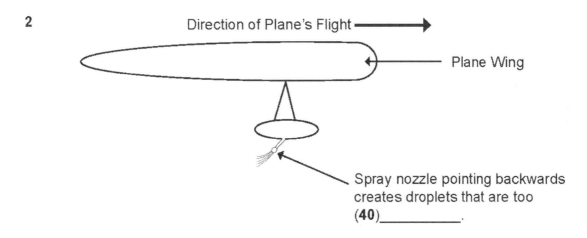

2

Direction of Plane's Flight ➞

Plane Wing

Spray nozzle pointing backwards creates droplets that are too (40)_____.

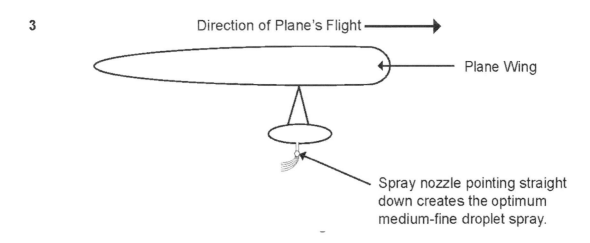

3

Direction of Plane's Flight ➞

Plane Wing

Spray nozzle pointing straight down creates the optimum medium-fine droplet spray.

READING

SECTION 1 *Questions 1 – 14*

Questions 1 – 7

Answer the questions below.

*Write **NO MORE THAN THREE WORDS AND/OR A NUMBER** from the text for each answer.*

*Write your answers in boxes **1 - 7** on your answer sheet.*

1   Who will open the celebrations for the anniversary day?

2   When will the town centre shops close on the anniversary day?

3   What organisation will receive any profit that is made at the anniversary day?

4   Who will be playing music in the afternoon of the anniversary day?

5   What will be the last event of the anniversary day?

6   How can people get home at the end of the anniversary day?

7   Who will be on duty to make sure people aren't too loud in the evening of the anniversary day?

Our Town's Anniversary Day Celebrations

In order to celebrate our town's 200th anniversary of being founded, we have planned a series of events to take place on Saturday 8th July. We hope that lots of people and their families will join us in the town centre for a day of fun and festivity. Children are of course very welcome and we hope that there will be plenty to fun things to do for the young and not so young.

The day will start at 11 a.m., when the town Mayor will formally launch the anniversary celebration with a short speech in the town gardens. She will be joined by the various councillors from the town council and some officials from the sponsors of the celebrations. The ceremony is planned to take only around 15 or 20 minutes, so please turn out especially to watch the opening ceremony so that you can support the sponsors who are paying for most of the fun all through the day.

The Mayor will spend all day in the town, wandering around to meet and talk to residents. Please don't ask her anything too serious, as the day is meant to be light-hearted! All the town centre's shops will be open and their normal closing time of 7 p.m. will be extended to 9 p.m., so the shopaholics amongst you can have the time of your lives. Do check though with stores outside the town centre for their planned opening and closing times.

In the town square from noon, there will be a fete, with lots of games to play for the young and not so young. Everything is either free or very cheap, so have a go at everything - please take note though of any age limits on any of the fun rides available. If there is any excess revenue left at the end of the day, the money will ALL go to the Children's Hospital. The entertainment is bound to be very popular, so please keep an eye on your children with all the crowds. We don't want any youngsters getting lost.

If you're hungry at any time, head for the town gardens, where a variety of different foods and drinks will be on sale. Feel free to sit on the grass and eat your food with your friends and family, but please use the rubbish bins for your waste. Most of the food providers will have microwaves and they will welcome any requests to warm up baby food.

In the late afternoon from 4.30 p.m., there will also be music to listen to in the town gardens. There will be various bands playing and everyone should find something to their taste. Lots of tables will be set up, so grab a place and a drink and relax. The music will end shortly before the firework display.

At 10 p.m., there will be a firework display to end the day's fun. The best places to see will be from the town gardens again or from Bellbottom Hill. Make sure you get a place to view early, as this will surely be a popular event. Please check that you haven't left any rubbish when you leave. Extra rubbish bins will be provided for any of your waste. People will be able to get back to their respective suburbs by night bus, and plenty of these will be laid on for free from 11 p.m. for one hour.

We hope you have a great day out. It will be a great opportunity for all of our town residents to get together and celebrate the anniversary of our beautiful town. All we ask is that you keep the town centre tidy and that you don't make too much noise heading home in the evening - the town centre's residents may be trying to get to sleep! Special constables will be on hand to watch over everything or to answer any questions that you might have, but we hope that they won't be needed.

Questions 8 – 14

Do the following statements agree with the information given in the text?

*In boxes **8 – 14** on your answer sheet write:*

TRUE   *if the statement agrees with the information*

FALSE   *if the statement contradicts the information*

NOT GIVEN   *if there is no information on this*

8   You must successfully take a theory test before being eligible for a learner licence.

9   Learner plates must be kept on a learner's car until they have had a full licence for 6 months.

10   Any 17-year-old with a learner licence can apply for a restricted licence.

11   There are validity limits for restricted licences.

12   Any holder of a current full New Zealand car licence can be a supervisor for a restricted licence driver.

13   Full licences can only be obtained after a driver has passed his/her eighteenth birthday.

14   The advanced driving skills course can be conducted only after a full licence has been held for at least 6 months.

Driving in New Zealand

There are three stages to getting a car licence. At each stage, you earn a new licence with fewer restrictions and more responsibilities.

Stage 1: learner licence

You must be at least 16 years old before you can apply for your learner licence and you first have to pass a road theory exam before you can get it. Your learner licence will be issued for five years and while on a learner licence:

- You must only drive with a supervisor sitting beside you at all times. Your supervisor must hold a current full New Zealand car licence, which does not have a supervisor condition. They must have held their full New Zealand licence (or an equivalent overseas licence) for at least two years.
- Your car must display learner (L) plates front and rear.
- You may carry passengers, but your supervisor has to agree to this.
- You face severe penalties if you drive outside the licence conditions.

Stage 2: restricted licence

To apply for your restricted licence, you must be at least 16½ years old and have held your learner licence for at least six months. To progress to this step, you'll have to pass a practical test of your driving skills. Your restricted licence will be issued for five years and while on a restricted licence:

- You can drive on your own, but not between 10 p.m. and 5 a.m.
- Generally, you cannot carry passengers without the supervision of a licensed car driver. Your supervisor must hold a current full New Zealand car licence that does not have a supervisor condition. They must have held their full New Zealand licence (or an equivalent overseas licence) for at least two years.

Stage 3: full licence

You must be at least 18 years of age before you can apply for your full licence. If you have completed an approved advanced driving skills course, this is reduced to 17½.
If you are under 25 years of age, you can apply after you've held your restricted licence for at least 18 months, or at least 12 months if you have completed an approved advanced driving skills course.
If you are 25 years of age or older, you can apply after you have held your restricted licence for at least six months, or at least three months if you have completed an approved advanced driving skills course.
To progress to a full licence, you have to pass a practical test by demonstrating safe driving behaviour across a wide range of traffic situations and road conditions.

It's important to prepare properly for all the above stages of getting a New Zealand driving licence. There are many licensed and approved driving schools all around the country and you are advised to take a number of lessons and only apply for a test when your instructor feels that you are ready to do so.

For details on how and where you can apply for a New Zealand driving licence and for how and where the relevant tests can be taken, please consult the New Zealand Transport Agency website.

SECTION 2   *Questions 15 – 27*

Questions 15 – 21

Complete the notes below.

Write **NO MORE THAN THREE WORDS** for each answer.

Write your answers in boxes **15 - 21** on your answer sheet.

Greening Ltd. – *notes for agency workers*

* The notes are for all agency workers (not workers who are (**15**) _____).

* Agency workers' contracts are not with Greening Ltd. Their agency will also clarify any work details with Greening Ltd.

* The working day is 8 a.m. – 5 p.m. (1 hour for lunch).

* New agency workers must go to the (**16**) _____ to get their assignments from Mr. Buckley.

* Departmental managers will inform agency workers about their duties and (**17**) _____ .

The Rights of Agency Workers at Greening Ltd.	
From Day 1	* Access to all facilities + notification of all (**18**) _____ .
After 12 Weeks	* The same basic conditions of employment as all Greening employees. * All pay rights (with some exclusions). * Working time rights, such as annual leave.
Note Bene	The 12 weeks begin again in various conditions, including starting work of greater (**19**) _____ at Greening Ltd.

* (**20**) _____ can be attended with pay by all agency workers.

* The (**21**) _____ is available for consultations if required.

Greening Ltd. – notes for agency workers

Welcome to Greening Ltd. These notes are meant to help any agency workers who are assigned to us. We hope that you enjoy your time with us and that it is profitable for both you and the company. These notes do not cover people who are self-employed. Self-employed workers should ask their contact point with Greening Ltd. for their terms and conditions of any employment with us.

Agency workers will not have contracts with Greening Ltd. When you're offered a job with Greening Ltd., the agency must tell you your start date, how long the work is likely to last, the type of work, about any expenses you may have to pay, the location, your hours, about any health and safety risks and about any experience, training or qualifications needed for the role. Some of these conditions may change after you have worked at Greening Ltd. for longer than 12 weeks (see below).

The working day at Greening Ltd. begins at 8 a.m. On their first day, all agency workers should report by 8 a.m. to Mr. Buckley, who is to be found in the personnel department. Mr. Buckley will tell you which department you are assigned to. When you get to your department, your department manager will tell you about your duties. The working day finishes at 5 p.m. All agency workers are allowed an hour for their lunch break and they are also entitled to morning and afternoon breaks. Your department manager will tell you the break times in your department.

All agency workers have certain rights according to law and the Greening Employee Charter.

From day one of their employment, any agency worker will be entitled to:

- the same rights to facilities such as staff canteens, childcare and transport as a comparable employee of the hirer.
- be informed about any job vacancies.

After a 12-week qualifying period, any agency worker will be entitled to the same basic conditions of employment as if they had been directly employed by Greening Ltd. This includes:

- pay - including any fee, bonus, commission, or holiday pay relating to the assignment. (It does not include redundancy pay, contractual sick pay, and maternity, paternity or adoption pay).
- working time rights - for example, including any annual leave above what is required by law.

Your 12 weeks will start again if you get a new job at a different workplace, have a break of more than 6 weeks between jobs at Greening Ltd., or stay at Greening Ltd. but take a new role that has more substantial responsibility. This kind of role is one that's completely new, different work. It could be a combination of different skills, pay rate, location, or working hours, or it could require new training.

All agency workers, regardless of how long they have been with Greening Ltd., will also be entitled to paid time off to go to ante-natal appointments during their working hours.

All agency workers are welcome to talk with the trade union representative (Mrs. White in the post room on the 4th floor) with regard to their rights and obligations.

Questions 22 – 27

Complete the summary below.

*Write **NO MORE THAN TWO WORDS** from the text for each answer.*

*Write your answers in boxes **22 - 27** on your answer sheet.*

Starting a Business – *the advantages of renting premises*

The advantages of renting premises for a new business start with (**22**) _____, meaning you are not stuck with a property. The duration of the (**23**) _____ can also be negotiated to suit your requirements (length etc.). Renting involves fewer initial costs, with only a (**24**) _____to be paid before the monthly rent. You are also not vulnerable to (**25**) _____ fluctuations and only changes in rent will raise your monthly costs. Drops in property value will usually not affect you. Your only building responsibilities will probably be internal maintenance, although there will probably be a service charge levied. Both landlords and tenants of business premises have health and safety responsibilities for the staff in terms of property's facilities and environment. A (**26**) _____ must be carried out and acted upon. An EPC will be issued by the landlord and you can use it to improve the property's energy performance. Who pays for what ought to be in the (**27**) _____. Finally, renting conditions can be negotiated with the landlord.

Starting a Business – *the advantage of renting premises*

When you're starting out in a business, one of the initial decisions you will have to make is whether to buy or rent the premises in which you wish to conduct your business.

Buying business premises is a big commitment and it's important to consider carefully whether renting is a better option. Renting can firstly provide more flexibility for your business as it grows. You are not locked into property ownership and you can usually agree with your landlord the length of the lease that you require, or have a break clause included. This will let you end your occupation (usually on a specific date) if, for instance, you want to relocate.

Financially, renting can make good business sense. Upfront charges for leasing premises are often relatively low, though you will have to provide a deposit. But generally, renting ties up less capital than buying, freeing up cash that could be used elsewhere in the business. You are not exposed to interest rate rises, although your rent may rise periodically as a result of rent reviews. Always check to see how rent is reviewed before you sign the lease.

There is also less potential for unexpected financial shocks - unless you wish to sell the remaining term on your lease to someone else, falls in property value will not affect you. Also, you will have no concerns about Capital Gains Tax, unless you decide to sell your lease for a premium.

You may have less responsibility for the building if you rent rather than buy, although this will depend on the terms of your lease. You may have to look after maintenance inside the building, but external maintenance is more likely to be the responsibility of the landlord, particularly in multi-occupancy premises; you may, however, have to pay a service charge.

If you are a tenant in commercial property and employ staff, you must ensure the workplace meets a number of basic requirements under health and safety rules. These include ensuring the workplace temperature is appropriate, providing sufficient space, ventilation and lighting, providing suitable sanitation and washing facilities, providing drinking water, maintaining equipment and keeping the premises clean and free of waste. You must perform a risk assessment in the workplace and take steps to remove any hazards and potential risks. Your landlord will also have health and safety duties regarding the premises that you are renting and you should ensure that these responsibilities are being met.

If you rent commercial premises, the landlord must issue you with an Energy Performance Certificate (EPC). The EPC provides information on energy efficiency using A-G ratings. It also includes recommendations for improvement. Acting on the recommendations can help you cut energy consumption, save money on bills and help reduce carbon emissions. The advantage to a renter is that the landlord should pay for all or at least a part of any improvements that you feel will improve the energy performance of the building. These responsibilities though should be laid out in your rental contract.

Whatever a landlord has put into a draft contract, the important thing is that renting can also give you space for negotiation. You or your agent can negotiate any aspect of the lease, either at the start or, if you want to renew it, after the lease ends. The landlord will be keen to rent his/her property, as it will not bring him/her any income unoccupied, so don't be afraid to ask (or even insist) on things. Remember, you can always walk away and find a property or landlord that will give you what you want.

SECTION 3   *Questions 28 – 40*

Questions 28 – 33

*The text on the following pages has 6 paragraphs (**A – F**).*

Choose the correct heading for each paragraph from the list of headings below.

*Write the correct number, **i - ix**, in boxes **28 - 33** on your answer sheet.*

i	Fundraising
ii	Government Support
iii	A Developing Service
iv	A Global Issue
v	A Lesson from America
vi	Early Lifesavers and their Craft
vii	New Training Facilities
viii	Launching
ix	The Beginning of the RNLI

28	Paragraph A
29	Paragraph B
30	Paragraph C
31	Paragraph D
32	Paragraph E
33	Paragraph F

Saving People from the Sea

Paragraph A

Drowning claims an estimated 372,000 lives around the world each year. This is a conservative estimate and the actual number is likely to be much higher. More than 90 per cent of these drownings happen in low- and middle-income countries. Despite the scale of the problem, it is barely recognised and it's hard to believe that this is not yet a priority around the world. The UK-based Royal National Lifeboat Institution (RNLI) is working to change that. Working in partnership with others, they are expanding their international work to provide communities with the knowledge, equipment and skills to try to reduce this staggering loss of life.

Paragraph B

The islands of Britain and Ireland have always been at the mercy of the sea. In the early 19th century, there was an average of 1800 shipwrecks a year around the coasts of Great Britain, with many sailors drowned. This danger was a tolerated part of life on board. Rescue services did exist in some places – there are records of a rescue boat stationed in Liverpool from 1730. In Bamburgh, Northumberland, men from the local castle patrolled the shore on horseback, ready to go to sea in their 'unimmergible' coble – the first purpose-built lifeboat, designed by Lionel Lukin. A 1789 competition, run by a group of businessmen from Newcastle, sought designs for rescue boats. One of the entries, from William Wouldhave, was designed to self right. Boat builder Henry Greathead was asked to build a lifeboat combining the best features of Lukin's and Wouldhave's plans, and came up with a vessel called the Original. Within 20 years, he had built more than 30 of these lifeboats, and they were soon saving lives all around Great Britain.

Paragraph C

Sir William Hillary is credited with founding the Royal National Lifeboat Institution. After witnessing the destruction of dozens of ships from his home on the Isle of Man, and getting involved in rescue attempts himself, Hillary appealed to the Navy, the government and other 'eminent characters' for help in forming 'a national institution for the preservation of lives and property from shipwreck'. With the support of London Members of Parliament (MP) and businesses, the Institution was founded as a charity on 4 March 1824. Hillary in fact took part in a rescue himself in 1830, at the age of 60. The packet St George had foundered on rocks at the entrance to Douglas harbour. Hillary commanded the lifeboat and was even washed overboard with others of the lifeboat crew. Finally, however, everyone aboard the St George was rescued with no loss of life.

Paragraph D

When Sir William Hillary first issued his appeal to the British nation in 1823, he sent it out to the Navy and government. He gained great sympathy, but not much cash! It was MP Thomas Wilson who suggested asking wealthy philanthropists to support the fledgling lifeboat service. Obtaining money in 1824 was very successful, bringing in almost £10,000, but the impetus soon stagnated and, by 1849, income had dropped to £354. Efforts in the mid-19th century were focused on the wealthy, and it wasn't until the late 1880's that the RNLI realised how generous the general public could be. Following a tragic disaster in 1886, a public appeal was launched that raised £10,000 in 2 weeks. A little later, there was the first 'Lifeboat Saturday'. Bands, floats and lifeboats paraded through the streets of Manchester, followed by volunteers with collecting buckets and purses on poles. More than £5,000 was taken on the day, which was the first recorded example of a charity street collection.

Paragraph E

For the RNLI's first 100 years or so, lifeboats were mostly put to sea and brought in from their local beaches. In many communities, hauling the lifeboat was done by women, as most of the men were on board, though farmers often loaned their horses to help bear the weight. Lifeboats were frequently dragged for long distances before putting to sea to minimise the time at sea in rough conditions. In 1899, the lifeboat in the village of Lynmouth, Devon, was hauled 10 miles by a team of 50 to 60 people and 18 horses to go to the aid of a vessel in distress in another bay. These days, most large, all-weather lifeboats are designed to go to sea from a slipway, or to lie afloat. But leaving land from the beach is still common, especially with the smaller, inshore lifeboats. Specially adapted tractors are now used to do the hauling.

Paragraph F

The way in which the public uses the sea has changed dramatically since the RNLI's foundation. More individuals are using the water for leisure, so the RNLI has had to change accordingly. In 2001, RNLI lifeguards began patrolling some of the most popular beaches in England and now lifeguards patrol over 200 beaches around the UK, rescuing thousands of people every year and providing first aid and safety advice. This 'prevention-rather-than-cure' approach also helps the RNLI's Coastal Safety and Education teams save lives by preventing people from getting into danger in the first place. Also in 2001, the RNLI's first station on an inland waterway was established in Northern Ireland. Environmental change has increased demand too. The Flood Rescue Team was formed in 2000 to respond to floods anywhere in the UK or Ireland within 6 hours. The RNLI also has an international Flood Rescue Team that can deploy anywhere in the world within 24 hours.

Questions 34 – 37

*Complete each sentence with the correct ending (**A - G**) below.*

*Write the correct letter (**A - G**) in boxes **34 - 37** on your answer sheet.*

34   The official figure of people drowned around the world is

35   In the past, the danger of drowning was

36   The lifeboat named "The Original" was

37   The founder of the RNLI was

A   employed by the British navy.

B   motivated by seeing many shipwrecks where he lived.

C   probably grossly under-estimated.

D   more dangerous on navy ships.

E   a mixture of different designs.

F   never accepted by the British navy.

G   always an accepted part of a seafarer's life.

Questions 38 – 40

*Choose the correct letter **A, B, C or D**.*

*Write the correct letter in boxes **38 - 40** on your answer sheet.*

38   Focusing on the public for early funding of the RNLI was

     A   less successful than approaching the rich.
     B   advised by British government officials.
     C   not a strategy followed at first.
     D   the first strategy attempted.

39   Early life boats were often

     A   moored at sea to save time.
     B   moved on land before being released into the sea.
     C   crewed at sea by women when the men were away.
     D   crewed by the local military forces.

40   The RNLI service has evolved because

     A   its initial operating strategy was not financially sustainable.
     B   of its dependence on people donating money.
     C   people interact with the sea in a different way than before.
     D   it is run solely by volunteers.

WRITING

WRITING TASK 1

You should spend about 20 minutes on this task.

You are travelling next month to stay with a family you do not know as part of a language training course.

Write a letter to the family to introduce yourself. In your letter,

- **say when and how you will be arriving** ✓
- **tell the family a little about yourself**
- **ask about the type of food that the family eats**

You should write at least 150 words.

*You do **NOT** need to write any addresses. Begin your letter as follows:*

Dear Mr and Mrs Greene,

WRITING TASK 2

You should spend about 40 minutes on this task.

Write about the following topic:

Do you feel it is better for young people leaving school to study further at university or go straight into the workplace?

Give reasons for your answer and include any relevant examples from your knowledge or experience.

You should write at least 250 words.

SPEAKING

PART 1

- Can you tell me a little about your job or studies?
- Do you like the job or studies that you do at the moment? (Why/Why not?)
- Do you prefer to work or study in the morning or later in the day? (Why?)

Topic 1   Happiness
- What makes you happy?
- Does money make people happy?
- Do you think young people are the happiest people? (Why/Why not?)
- Why can pets make people happy?

Topic 2   Photography
- Do you like to take photographs? (Why/Why not?)
- Why do you think people like to keep photographs?
- Can taking photographs be an invasion of people's privacy? (Why?)
- What are the dangers of having photographs taken today with regards to the Internet?

PART 2

Describe a memorable teacher.
You should say:
        who this teacher was
        what this teacher taught
        where you knew this teacher
and briefly explain why this teacher is so memorable.

PART 3

Topic 1   Teachers
- What are the qualities that make a good teacher?
- Do you think that teachers are underpaid for what they do?
- What are the main challenges facing teachers today?
- What can governments do to improve the job that teachers have to do?

Topic 2   Education and Schools
- How do you think education has changed over the last 50 years?
- What role do parents have in their children's education?
- Do you think that private education is something that should be allowed in today's society? (Why/Why not?)
- Should education be delivered to single- or mixed-sex classes? (Why/Why not?)

PRACTICE TEST 15

LISTENING

 Download audio recordings for the test here:
https://www.ielts-blog.com/ielts-practice-tests-downloads/

PART 1   *Questions 1 – 10*

Questions 1 – 6

Complete the hospital's new employee record sheet below.

Write **NO MORE THAN THREE WORDS AND/OR A NUMBER** *from the listening for each answer.*

New Employee Record Sheet

Applicant's Name:	Adam (**1**) _____
Address:	82 Ackland Road Gorley
Postcode:	OG8 6RE
Mobile Telephone:	07543 842 (**2**) _____
National Insurance Number:	MA 67 95 36 F
Age:	(**3**) _____
Times Available:	6 a.m. - 9 a.m. & after 3 p.m. - 10 p.m. (**4**) _____ at weekends
Experience:	Weekend job at a nearby (**5**) _____ - washed up, cleaned surfaces and floors David at david@apple.com can provide us with a (**6**) _____

Questions 7 – 10

Complete Adam's notes below.

*Write **NO MORE THAN TWO WORDS** from the listening for each answer.*

When I arrive and leave, I need to sign in and out at the (**7**) _____ for employees - this ensures my work times and pay are correct. I get £9 an hour.

In the staff changing rooms, I must change into overalls and a (**8**) _____.

Every 3 hours I get a break - I can go outside or go to the (**9**) _____, where I can get a drink; if I work longer than 4 hours, I get a meal.

I will start next Saturday at 9 a.m.

I need to come in as well for a bit of (**10**) _____ on Thursday at 4 p.m. (I'll be paid for this).

PART 2   Questions 11 - 20

Questions 11 – 16

Complete the summary below on the radio talk on the town exhibition.

*Write **NO MORE THAN TWO WORDS AND/OR A NUMBER** from the listening for each answer.*

The Town Exhibition

The town exhibition will be found in the (**11**) _____ of the town from the 9th July to the 14th July. The exhibition firstly is a show for local businesses, especially for apple products. Secondly, the exhibition is a town fair, with lots of games and amusements. The latter mainly starts from (**12**) _____ p.m. The exhibition ends nightly with a fireworks display at 10 p.m., which is at the central lake. This final show can often upset (**13**) _____, so it's best to leave them behind. There will be plenty of international food and drinks on offer and an open fire barbecue offering freshly grilled meats and (**14**) _____.

Please dress children suitably and don't forget sun cream and a hat if it's sunny. In bad weather, don't forget raincoats and umbrellas; consider wearing (**15**) _____, which will help if it's very muddy.

There will be a lottery every evening, with results given just before the fireworks. Tickets are a dollar for 4. Write your name and (**16**) _____ on the back of your tickets if you can't stay for the results.

Questions 17 – 20

Below is a plan of the town exhibition with 6 locations marked A - F.

Questions 17 - 20 name 4 places that can be visited at the exhibition.

Write the correct letter (A - F) that matches the places that can be visited with their locations.

17	Exhibition on other local businesses	_____
18	The first aid station	_____
19	Food stations	_____
20	Amusement rides	_____

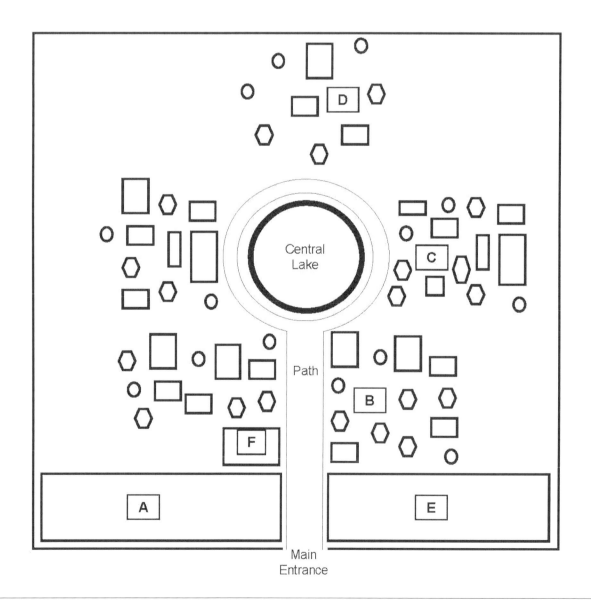

PART 3   *Questions 21 – 30*

Questions 21 – 25

*Choose the correct letter **A, B, or C**.*

21   Two years ago, the US had to import approximately

    A   a third of its petroleum needs.
    B   half of its petroleum needs.
    C   three quarters of its petroleum needs.

22   Generating electricity on board a car is not usually done, because

    A   onboard generators are too heavy.
    B   onboard generators are too bulky.
    C   it's not an economic way of powering a car.

23   Electric cars have cheaper fuel costs mainly because

    A   conventional fuel is more expensive than electricity.
    B   electric cars are lighter than conventional cars.
    C   electric cars are slower than conventional cars.

24   Electric cars' lifecycle emissions depend on

    A   the type of electric motor used in the cars.
    B   where in the US the electricity used for power is generated.
    C   the speed at which the cars are driven.

25   Biofuel B100's emissions are compensated for by

    A   the lack of carbon dioxide that is generated by the biodiesel engine.
    B   the number people who have switched to using the fuel.
    C   the growth of the source plants for the fuel.

Questions 26 – 30

Complete the table below.

Write **NO MORE THAN TWO WORDS** from the listening for each answer.

The Disadvantages of Electric Cars	
Refuelling Infrastructure	* Not as common as gas stations * Relevant organisations are expanding the network * Potentially available anywhere people park * Hybrids can use a (**26**) _____ when necessary
Purchase Costs	* Much higher than conventional cars * Prices will drop as (**27**) _____ grow * Purchase costs can be offset by fuel savings, tax credits and state (**28**) _____
Maintenance	* Similar to conventional cars, except the battery * Batteries will wear out in spite of their design for extended life * Some manufacturers offer different types of (**29**) _____ for batteries * Battery life a big disadvantage - can be expensive to replace * Improvements in (**30**) _____ and greater manufacturing output will lead to lower battery prices

PART 4   Questions 31 – 40

Questions 31 – 40

*Complete the notes below. Write **NO MORE THAN TWO WORDS** from the listening for each answer.*

Twin Languages

Twin languages are officially called autonomous languages; not a (**31**) _____ event - occurs in approx. 40% of twins.

<u>Formulation</u>

Because twins are so close, they don't communicate so much with others and they develop their own communication system.
It's not always between twins - it's evident also in close siblings.
It usually occurs with the lack of exposure to grown up (**32**) _____ speech.
Autonomous languages usually consist of onomatopoeic utterances, some (**33**) _____ and normal language adapted by children within their speech limitations.
Autonomous languages lack morphology and have a strange word order.
Autonomous languages are hard for other people to understand.

<u>Research</u>

Only (**34**) _____ can explain how and why autonomous languages emerge.
Autonomous languages could arise in children with phonology delays due to little or no language sources to copy.
Children normally develop speech in the same way and make the same (**35**) _____ when talking.
Phonological delays can produce similar language to a "twin language".
Autonomous languages can be (**36**) _____ in twins and close siblings as they communicate in a similar way.
(**37**) _____ is often needed to help with sound development.
Autonomous languages have also been linked to language delays at school.

<u>Parents</u>

Parents needn't worry too much - children can switch between secret and normal languages.
Not all children using an autonomous language will have language delays.
An autonomous language is a (**38**) _____ for speech and language problems - a therapist would probably be helpful.
Parents are the best guide for children's language - they influence sound development and the children's length of (**39**) _____.
Parents should therefore talk as much as possible to their children.
(**40**) _____ is very beneficial for all children, especially twins.

<u>Conclusion</u>

Autonomous languages usually disappear after intervention or interaction with other children at school.
Children might occasionally revert to the autonomous language (normal), but with care, this will not lead to language problems.

READING

SECTION 1   *Questions 1 – 14*

Questions 1 – 7

Complete the sentences below.

*Write **NO MORE THAN THREE WORDS** from the text for each answer.*

*Write your answers in boxes **1 - 7** on your answer sheet.*

1   At the year group stations, visitors will be able to see _____ as well as talk to students and staff.

2   The _____ will speak to visitors and address any queries.

3   Visitors are advised to check with the school _____ before coming.

4   Visitors are advised to inform their _____, so they know which children will be absent.

5   Visitors are encouraged to send the school _____, so the school can improve the next Open Day.

6   Visitors are advised that a _____ visit is best.

7   Visitors are requested to keep _____ to a minimum during lesson visits.

Riverside Secondary School Open Day

Next month, on the first Monday of the month, Riverside Secondary School will hold its annual Open Day. During this day, we aim to show present and prospective parents and students our school during a normal working day. Pupils will show you around and you'll be able to visit classrooms, and speak to teachers and students. Throughout the whole day, there will be all-day presentations in the sports hall. Each school year and each subject group will have a station manned by staff and students. Prospective parents and students will be able to find all the information they want from those on duty and they'll also be able to examine sample work studied by all the years studying at the school. The year 6 station will be the largest and have the most staff and students on duty to give information. This is because the largest intake annually is into this year group. If you see the station you're interested in is particularly busy, go for a walk and see something else rather than spending a long time waiting in line.

At 11 a.m., there will be a short talk by our head of marketing and this will be followed by a short questions – answers session. At lunchtime, there will be a section of the school cafeteria cordoned off for visitors and you can try out the food that our students and staff eat every day. There will be vegetarian and vegan options available. Please inform our serving personnel of any allergies you might have.

DOs

DO bring your child – he or she will be the one attending the school

DO prepare some questions for students and teachers

DO look over our website first, so that you don't ask unnecessary questions

DO tell your primary school that you and your child are attending our Open Day

DO spend a meaningful amount of time on your visit

DO provide us with feedback on the day, so we can make it better next year

DO try the food and see what your child will be eating

DON'Ts

DON'T judge the school by any individual students or teachers

DON'T get too fixed on details – try and get an overall view of the school

DON'T come too late – the morning is always the most useful time

DON'T bring the whole extended family – the day will get too crowded

DON'T make too much noise in class time

DON'T just stay in one classroom the whole time – move around

Questions 8 – 14

*The text on the following page offers different pieces of advice, **A – K**, on writing a covering letter.*

Which piece of advice contains the following information?

*Write the correct letter, **A - K**, in boxes **8 - 14** on your answer sheet.*

8   Make sure the covering letter is customised to the company and job applied for.

9   Make sure you mention any relevant training that you have had.

10   Ensure the writing style in your covering letter is not too relaxed.

11   Make sure your letter is prepared and printed from a laptop or PC.

12   Make sure you proofread your covering letter before sending it.

13   Find out from the company who the letter should be addressed to.

14   If the company requires an application to be submitted by email, make sure that you've included all the necessary documentation.

Writing a Covering Letter – Top Tips

When making nearly all job applications today, you are expected to also send a covering letter. As your prospective employer is very likely to read this letter before they get to your CV, it's important that you make an effort to make a good impression with it. Here are some hints to creating an effective covering letter.

A   Use a computer to write your covering letter. This is what will be expected and, while a hand-written letter may seem more personal, it will seem strange nowadays. It also makes the letter easier to edit before you send it and to be read.

B   Personalise your letter. While it's a temptation to use one letter for all applications when you're filling in a lot, a letter tailored to the job on offer is much more likely to make a positive impact on the employer. It also stops you including details of other job applications, which will destroy your chances of success.

C   Your letter should focus on your strengths and achievements, but try not to just repeat all the details of your CV.

D   Use the right tone. A job application should be formal, business-like and polite. The letter should also be checked for grammar and spelling errors, and should use the same text format and font size throughout. All these things will signal your professionalism.

E   Don't go on – about five paragraphs over two sides should be enough. Employers often have many applications to screen and they don't want to (and probably won't) read eight sides.

F   Do some research. Don't just send the letter off to the company. Call the company and find who will be reading it and direct it to him/her. It's easily noticed that you know what you're applying for and it will make you look good in the eyes of anyone reading your covering letter. Make sure you include at the top of the letter the job title, job reference number (if there is one) and where you saw the advertisement.

G   The start. The first paragraph is where you will grab attention. Make sure that you show your keenness for the job and why you are the right person for it.

H   The middle. Target the skills required for the job and show how your experience, qualifications and personal qualities make you a match for it. Emphasise any job-appropriate education or course certificates you have. Show your willingness to learn new skills and work with new people.

I   Sign off. Do it in a professional way and say how you'd like to be contacted (your contact details should be in your CV).

J   If you're sending the application by electronic mail, don't forget to attach your covering letter and CV. Everyone forgets sometimes, but it doesn't create a good impression when applying for a job!

K   Be formal. Of course it's important to have friendly staff, but people expect high formality in job applications. It's the same for an interview. You wouldn't turn up for an interview in jeans and a T-shirt!

SECTION 2   *Questions 15 – 27*

Questions 15 – 20

Answer the questions below.

Write **NO MORE THAN THREE WORDS AND/OR A NUMBER** *from the text for each answer.*

Write your answers in boxes **15 - 20** *on your answer sheet.*

15   What kind of rotating shift schedules are best for minimising employees' fatigue?

16   What is the maximum length of a night shift at the company?

17   Where can employees find details on work carried out to make the night time work environment safer?

18   Who will make taxi reservations on behalf of company employees?

19   What kind of workers are not covered by the company night working rules?

20   Who were consulted when creating the health assessment questionnaire?

Notes for Employees Considering Night Time Working

Due to the nature of our business, it's sometimes necessary that our staff work at night.

Night shifts can be particularly demanding on employee wellbeing and health. This can include disruption to the body clock, fatigue, sleeping difficulties, disturbed appetite and digestion, reliance on sedatives or stimulants, social and domestic problems and other symptoms of ill health. To combat this, we do not have employees on night shifts for extended periods. This is because workers' bodies will just have started to adapt to the new pattern. We find rotation shifts every two to three days are best for workers and weekly or fortnightly rotations are the least comfortable for workers. Forward-rotating programs (moving from morning to afternoon to night shifts) are better than backward-rotating ones in terms of sleep loss and tiredness.

If someone works at night, there are rules covering the hours they work. Night time working hours are usually between 11 p.m. and 6 a.m. - but this can be flexible and should be discussed between you and us. To qualify as night working, the night time period must be no more than 8 hours and include the period between midnight and 5 a.m. Any of our staff under 18 years are not allowed to be night workers.

We must make sure that you don't work more than an average of 8 hours in a 24-hour period. By law, you can't opt out of this working limit. We must also keep records of any night workers' working hours to prove they aren't exceeding night working limits, and we must keep the records for at least 2 years. These records can be inspected by you at any time.

Another legal requirement for night work is that we conduct a risk assessment. We must identify any hazards in your work, assess how harmful they could be and take steps to reduce any risks. We conduct regular risk assessments for our night workers and the environment in which they work. The latest risk assessment and the action report on work to address any issues is always available.

If you work any shift for us that ends between 11.00 p.m. and 06.00 a.m., we will pay the cost of a taxi to the worker's home. The company has a contract with a local taxi service and employees must use this company, as we have secured good discounts because of our regular use. Because of the ongoing contract, employees are not required pay in the taxi now or keep any receipts. Please ask the company secretary before lunch on the day of travel, so that you can get an assured booking. Regular night workers should contact the company secretary to give him/her details of their shift before it starts, so that a regular booking can be made. Employees living near each other will be required to share taxis in order to cut costs.

Our usual limits and regulations for night workers do not apply to the self-employed working with us. This does not include agency workers, who are treated as normal workers with us.

If you agree to working at night for us, the agreement will be put in writing.

If you are to begin working at night, we must perform a health assessment before you become a night worker and on a regular basis after that. Usually, this is just done with a series of questions, which was created in collaboration with health professionals. If there are any health questions regarding your fitness for night work, we will offer you a supplemental examination by a medical professional if you still wish to do nights.

Questions 21 – 27

Do the following statements agree with the information given in the text?

*In boxes **21 – 27** on your answer sheet write:*

> **TRUE**   *if the statement agrees with the information*
> **FALSE**   *if the statement contradicts the information*
> **NOT GIVEN**   *if there is no information on this*

21   For a lot of companies, backing up data should not be an expensive process.

22   Management should provide regular training on recommended back up practices.

23   Employees destroying data on purpose is unusual.

24   Responsibility for backing up data should be shared amongst all relevant staff members.

25   Backing up its material on a cloud system can save a company the time and money spent backing up things on other hardware.

26   Using best practice for back ups can usually keep back up material free from viruses.

27   Viruses usually infect company systems because of employees opening infected emails.

Advice on Backing up Data

Protecting your IT systems and business data is vitally important. Business information can be a valuable asset, and critical information such as financial data and customer records can be very difficult to replace. Loss of confidential or sensitive data can also have serious consequences. In most situations, small investments of time and money can achieve large improvements in information security. Often, security can be improved by simple common sense and good management practice.

The extensive use of computer systems makes business operations vulnerable to major problems, ranging from the accidental loss of data to deliberate sabotage by staff (though the latter is very rare). Storage systems, whether computer or paper-based, can also be at risk of theft or physical damage through a fire or flood.

A backup copy of your business data can allow you to continue trading, even if computer data has been lost. Backups can be made to portable media such as magnetic tapes, DVD-ROMs or external hard drives. Alternatively, online backup services allow you to back up your data over the Internet to the service provider's data storage facility.

A common way today to back up important data is to use a cloud service. Once set up, this can be a low stress and low management option for keeping all information safe. There are, however, a few things to bear in mind. First of all, you should ensure that the processing carried out by your cloud service provider complies with the data protection act. The best way to do this is to have a contract and a data processing agreement in place. Secondly, when choosing your cloud service provider, you should select a data processor providing sufficient guarantees about the technical and organisational security measures governing the processing to be carried out, and that they must take reasonable steps to ensure compliance with those measures. Thirdly, you should research your cloud service provider's record in providing service availability. Service availability means ensuring timely and reliable access to personal data. One threat to availability in the cloud that is often outside the responsibility of the cloud service provider is the accidental loss of network connectivity between you and the service provider. You should therefore check whether they have adopted reasonable measures to cope with the risk of disruptions such as backup Internet network links.

You should have a backup routine (typically daily) as part of your IT security policy and you should check that this is being correctly carried out.

Best practice for backing up data includes:

- giving one person the main duty for backing up, and designating a second to cover for absence
- not relying solely on a cloud-based backup system for keeping your data safe
- using a different tape, external hard drive or disk to back up each day of the week and having a schedule for rotating them – this can nearly always safeguard backups in the case of a malware attack or the like
- keeping backups secure - preferably off-site from the main business premises, e.g. in a bank box
- periodically testing your backups to ensure that your data can be successfully restored

Data backups are a key part of business continuity planning for IT systems.

SECTION 3   *Questions 28 – 40*

*Read the following passage and answer Questions **28 – 40**.*

The Blue Whale

The blue whale is the largest animal in the world. A female blue whale weighing 150 tons (killed in the Antarctic in 1928) was the largest animal ever known to have lived during the Earth's 4600 million-year history.

The body statistics of a blue whale are amazing. Marine biologist, Ariadne Scott, describes them. "An average individual is 21 metres long and weighs 100 tons. It has almost 2,500 gallons of blood and burns up to 3 million calories a day. Its heart weighs more than a ton and the tongue alone weighs about 2 tons." The life expectancy of the blue whale is harder to judge, although they are known to be among Earth's longest-lived animals. Scientist, Sophie Morton, explains how whale experts try and work out their age. "We have discovered that by counting the layers of a deceased whale's wax-like earplugs, we can get a close estimate of the animal's age. The oldest blue whale found using this method was determined to be around 110 years old and we estimate that average lifespan is estimated at around 80 to 90 years."

Blue whales are also the loudest animals on Earth, with their calls reaching 188 decibels (a jet reaches 140 decibels). Recently, Australian marine scientists have detected individuals singing from almost 750 kilometres away. Although no one is certain, the blue whale calls are theorised to be probably a part of breeding behaviour. The Australian scientists can use the data they found for various uses. Australian Science Leader, Dr Mike Dance, said, "Using innovative advanced echosounders, we were able to track individual krill for the first time, allowing an examination of the changing internal structure of the krill swarms that blue whales prey upon. Our ability to find these blue whales also allowed us to investigate the whales' habitat."

This enormous animal is a real gentle giant. The blue whale is a baleen, which means it feeds only on krill, a small shrimp-like crustacean. Its stomach can hold one ton of krill and it needs to eat about four tons of krill each day. The blue whale spends its summers following its prey and building up its fat reserves, but, as wildlife expert Jon Stephens explains, things change in winter. "Summers are spent in polar waters, because food production is higher there, but in winter, they migrate several thousand miles to warmer tropic and subtropic areas and fast for the duration of their stay while breeding, using the fat on their bodies to see them through the whole winter." Blue whales usually only congregate for this reproduction and they do not live in the pods common for other whale species. They are found in small numbers throughout the world's oceans, except the Mediterranean and the Arctic.

Conservationist Patrick Liley explains why the blue whale fat is one factor that has threatened the blue whale. "Historically, hunters have chased them to harvest their meat and render the cold-resistant fat down to oil. The larger the whale, the more profit is made from a kill. Killing blue whales therefore made the most commercial sense." The blue whale is currently one of the world's most endangered whales. It was not hunted until modern techniques made them more easily attainable, but by the mid-1900's, only about 1,000 were estimated to remain.

Blue whales have been protected from whaling since 1966 by the International Whaling Commission, though some were hunted unlawfully until 1972. Stocks in the Southern Hemisphere and North Pacific are currently recovering. The latest estimate revealed 15,000 blue whales remaining worldwide, while pre-whaling populations were estimated at perhaps 300,000 individuals. Although numbers are increasing, worries remain of the health of the population. New Zealand fisheries spokesman, Alan Cook, explains. "It is not known whether the population is properly recovering. There is a real concern that the drastically depleted genetic pool created by the hunting will affect their capacity to breed properly. Only time will tell if the figures continue to grow."

Other threats to the blue whale include their involvement in other forms of fishing, climate change and destruction or modification of habitat. Fisheries Inspector, Steve Hartnett, describes the threat from fishing. "Like many marine animals, blue whales are at risk of 'bycatch', which is accidental entanglement in fishing gear, which can cause injury, infections, starvation and drowning." Climate change may also affect blue whales throughout the Southern Hemisphere by depleting or shifting the distribution of prey. Melting ice also allows oil companies better accessibility to oil and gas deposits. This can cause various problems for blue whales and their environment, including one that is not often considered. Alice Baggley, an environment spokesperson, explains the problem. "There is concern that noise pollution may affect blue whales' ability to communicate, particularly in New Zealand, where there is persistent seismic activity for oil and gas extraction near a blue whale foraging ground."

The blue whale is the largest animal to have lived on the Earth. Like many creatures, human activities threaten its continued existence. Patrick Liley explains what he feels is the solution. "It's not a secret. Whaling caused the initial destruction of the blue whale, and it continues to do so. We need to make all countries stop whaling and close the loophole on 'whaling for scientific purposes' that permits commercial whaling to carry on."

Questions 28 – 35

Look at the following statements (questions 28 - 35) and the list of people below.

Match each statement with the correct person's initials.

Write the correct initials in boxes 28 - 35 on your answer sheet.

28   Damage to blue whale numbers may have damaged the whales' ability to reproduce in a sustainable way.

29   A dead blue whale was used to estimate how long blue whales live.

30   What helps blue whales survive winters has led to them being attractive targets for whalers.

31   New technology has helped research the food that blue whales eat.

32   The blue whale's dimensions are extraordinary.

33   Countries exploiting gaps in the whaling law need to be stopped to halt the threat to blue whales.

34   Blue whales do not feed during their periods of mating.

35   Hydrocarbon fuel exploration could affect how blue whales communicate with each other.

AS	Ariadne Scott
SM	Sophie Morton
MD	Mike Dance
JS	Jon Stephens
PL	Patrick Liley
AC	Alan Cook
SH	Steve Hartnett
AB	Alice Baggley

Questions 36 – 40

*Choose the correct letter **A, B, C or D**.*

*Write the correct letter in boxes **36 - 40** on your answer sheet.*

36　　Scientists are now fairly certain that blue whale sounds

　　A　　help coordinate hunting krill.
　　B　　help during the mating period.
　　C　　help whales coordinate migration.
　　D　　help echo-location in shallow water.

37　　Blue whales gather in groups

　　A　　in colder polar waters.
　　B　　when hunting krill in polar waters.
　　C　　to make them safer from shark or killer whale attacks.
　　D　　when they want to breed.

38　　The blue whale only became endangered

　　A　　once hunting methods developed to make it easy to succeed.
　　B　　once the early ban on them was lifted.
　　C　　once the polar ice began to melt.
　　D　　once world demand increased.

39　　Although blue whales should not have been subject to hunting since its abolition,

　　A　　their numbers have continued to drop.
　　B　　some illegal hunting continued for a while.
　　C　　new breeding proved to be a problem.
　　D　　hunting technology continued to improve.

40　　Blue whales getting accidentally caught up in fishermen's nets

　　A　　gives fishermen an unexpected financial bonus.
　　B　　can occur when the blue whale hunts the same prey as the fishermen.
　　C　　can cause blue whales to drown.
　　D　　can now be avoided using sonar.

WRITING

WRITING TASK 1

You should spend about 20 minutes on this task.

You would like to borrow a good camera from a friend.

Write a letter to your friend. In your letter,

- **ask your friend if you can borrow the camera**
- **explain why you want to borrow the camera**
- **say when you want it and when you will return it**

You should write at least 150 words.

*You do **NOT** need to write any addresses. Begin your letter as follows:*

Dear Roy,

WRITING TASK 2

You should spend about 40 minutes on this task.

Write about the following topic:

With the increase in computer use, many people feel that schools do not need to put the emphasis that they used to on basic handwriting skills or mental mathematics skills.

To what extent do you agree or disagree with this?

Give reasons for your answer and include any relevant examples from your knowledge or experience.

You should write at least 250 words.

SPEAKING

PART 1

- Where do you work/study?
- How do you travel to work/study?
- What is the best thing about your job/studies?

Topic 1　　Football
- Do you like football? (Why/Why not?)
- Why do you think football is so popular around the world?
- Why do you think so many people support their country or a particular team?
- Why do you think so much violence happens amongst people who watch football?

Topic 2　　Being in Another Country
- What is the most interesting foreign country that you have visited? (Why?)
- What kind of things do you do when you visit a different country?
- What are some of things that are surprising when you have gone to a different country?
- What are some of the problems that happen when two people from different countries marry?

PART 2

Describe your first mobile/cell phone.
You should say:
　　　　when you got this mobile/cell phone
　　　　how much it cost
　　　　what it looked like
and explain how different it is from the mobile/cell phone you use nowadays.

PART 3

Topic 1　　Mobile/Cell Phones
- How have mobile phones changed life today?
- Do you think the use of mobile phones is overpriced?
- How do you think mobile phones will change over the next 50 years?
- Do you think young people spend too much time and money on their mobile phones? (Why?)

Topic 2　　Technology
- What part of modern technology could you not do without today?
- Could you compare society's dependence on technology today with 50 years ago?
- What are some of the disadvantages of society's dependence on technology today?
- How will education systems have to change so that today's youth can use and improve today's technology?

Listening Test Answer Sheet

1		21	
2		22	
3		23	
4		24	
5		25	
6		26	
7		27	
8		28	
9		29	
10		30	
11		31	
12		32	
13		33	
14		34	
15		35	
16		36	
17		37	
18		38	
19		39	
20		40	

Reading Test Answer Sheet

1		21	
2		22	
3		23	
4		24	
5		25	
6		26	
7		27	
8		28	
9		29	
10		30	
11		31	
12		32	
13		33	
14		34	
15		35	
16		36	
17		37	
18		38	
19		39	
20		40	

Answers

LISTENING ANSWERS

/ indicates an alternative answer   ( ) indicates an optional answer

TEST 11	TEST 12	TEST 13	TEST 14	TEST 15
1. 6 months	1. B	1. Gloria	1. coaches	1. Marshall
2. email	2. B	2. 40	2. first aid	2. 592
3. photo	3. C	3. 451	3. sports complex	3. 21
4. 5%	4. C	4. Bank transfer	4. fruit	4. mornings
5. signature	5. A	5. cats	5. snacks	5. restaurant
6. E	6. hills	6. 8.30	6. 4.30	6. reference
7. A	7. bus	7. clothing	7. C	7. reception
8. D	8. 5	8. nurse	8. C	8. (special) hat
9. B	9. picnic	9. information pack	9. A	9. (staff) canteen
10. E	10. map	10. weekends	10. A	10. training
11. The town council	11. B*	11. 60	11. E	11. park
12. Every 6 months	12. E*	12. married couples	12. D	12. 3
13. The interactive classroom	13. A°	13. specialised diets	13. B	13. dogs
14. 3 hours	14. D°	14. independent	14. A	14. vegetables
15. 2 p.m.	15. F°	15. website	15. H	15. (rubber) boots
16. self-assessment test	16. D	16. guest	16. Opportunity	16. telephone number
17. bookkeeping	17. B	17. brain	17. locations	17. A
18. Computers for Photography	18. C	18. 1-day	18. signal	18. F
19. shortcuts	19. H	19. isolation	19. (user) manual	19. D
20. skills	20. A	20. (special) tools	20. brand	20. C
21. Broadband	21. D	21. B	21. tourism	21. A
22. bias	22. A	22. A	22. budget	22. C
23. notice (periods)	23. H	23. C	23. exchange rates	23. A
24. tariff(s) (information)	24. B	24. B	24. (import) duty	24. B
25. profit	25. G	25. C	25. taxes	25. C
26. signal	26. sand	26. Well head	26. transportation	26. fossil fuel
27. C	27. high tide	27. Cap rock	27. quality	27. production (volumes)
28. A	28. undercut	28. Underground sensors	28. biodiversity	28. incentives
29. statistical analysis	29. The coastguard	29. by satellite	29. water	29. warranty
30. cinema	30. mobile phones	30. 4 weeks	30. pest control	30. technology
31. decay	31. personality	31. influence	31. intervals	31. rare
32. standard of living	32. mean	32. subconscious	32. moist soil	32. model
33. 2	33. verbal	33. concentration	33. leaves	33. invented words
34. earthquakes	34. psychological	34. relaxation	34. revenue	34. situational factors
35. (active) volcanic zones	35. literacy	35. sense organs	35. machine	35. errors
36. steam	36. extreme ends	36. potential	36. (monetary) loan	36. prolonged
37. transient	37. interpretation	37. homework	37. protein	37. (Speech) therapy
38. high pressure	38. (brain) damage	38. C	38. a holding tank	38. risk factor
39. A local substation	39. school	39. E	39. slipstream	39. sentence
40. A cooling tower	40. reliability	40. G	40. coarse	40. Reading

*Note: Test 12, answers for qu. 11 + 12, and for qu. 13, 14 + 15 can be written in any order

READING ANSWERS

/ indicates an alternative answer   ( ) indicates an optional answer

TEST 11	TEST 12	TEST 13	TEST 14	TEST 15
1. D	1. anxiety	1. E	1. The town Mayor	1. (sample) work
2. C	2. email	2. B	2. 9 p.m.	2. head of marketing
3. B	3. blood	3. C	3. The Children's Hospital	3. website
4. C	4. medications	4. H	4. Various bands	4. primary school
5. B	5. anaesthetic	5. D	5. A firework display	5. feedback
6. A	6. blood circulation	6. C	6. by night bus	6. morning
7. D	7. checklist	7. D	7. Special constables	7. noise
8. FALSE	8. council tax	8. H	8. TRUE	8. B
9. TRUE	9. redirect	9. The head waiter	9. NOT GIVEN	9. H
10. NOT GIVEN	10. meters	10. A small deposit	10. FALSE	10. K
11. TRUE	11. window	11. The nurse	11. TRUE	11. A
12. FALSE	12. TRUE	12. Hotel residents	12. FALSE	12. D
13. TRUE	13. NOT GIVEN	13. In plastic receptacles	13. FALSE	13. F
14. NOT GIVEN	14. FALSE	14. (The) entertainment board	14. NOT GIVEN	14. J
15. tailored	15. The staff management	15. notice	15. self-employed	15. Forward-rotating programs
16. skills	16. loneliness	16. pay	16. personnel department	16. 8 hours
17. resign	17. Promotion	17. issues	17. break times	17. The action report
18. assessment	18. The employee's post	18. counter offer	18. job vacancies	18. The company secretary
19. relevance	19. A risk assessment	19. in lieu	19. responsibility	19. The self-employed
20. in-house	20. Overhead house lighting	20. reference	20. Ante-natal appointments	20. Health professionals
21. morale	21. prevention	21. responsibilities	21. trade union representative	21. TRUE
22. Shortcomings	22. bed	22. F	22. flexibility	22. NOT GIVEN
23. recycling facility	23. technique	23. B	23. lease	23. TRUE
24. regulations	24. breaks	24. I	24. deposit	24. FALSE
25. leftovers	25. commute	25. G	25. interest rate	25. FALSE
26. durability	26. fitness	26. C	26. risk assessment	26. TRUE
27. symbiosis	27. performance	27. A	27. rental contract	27. NOT GIVEN
28. scientific research	28. ix	28. TRUE	28. iv	28. AC
29. waterways	29. iv	29. NOT GIVEN	29. vi	29. SM
30. uninhabitable	30. v	30. TRUE	30. ix	30. PL
31. samples	31. ii	31. TRUE	31. i	31. MD
32. controversial	32. viii	32. FALSE	32. viii	32. AS
33. distances	33. vi	33. C	33. iii	33. PL
34. lasers	34. x	34. D	34. C	34. JS
35. range	35. B*	35. C	35. G	35. AB
36. FALSE	36. C*	36. B	36. E	36. B
37. FALSE	37. E*	37. A	37. B	37. D
38. NOT GIVEN	38. G*	38. timber posts	38. C	38. A
39. D	39. H*	39. earthed	39. B	39. B
40. C	40. C	40. more narrowly spaced	40. C	40. C

* Note: Test 12, answers for qu. 35, 36, 37, 38 + 39 can be written in any order

READING ANSWERS HELP

This section shows fragments of passages that contain the correct answers. If you have trouble locating the correct answer in the text, or can't understand why a particular answer is correct, refer to this section to understand the reasoning behind the answers. A group of answers with answers being preceded by * means that this group of answers may be given in any order. Answers in brackets () are optional answers.

GENERAL READING TEST 11

1. **D**   Drop into our offices or we can visit you in your house, offices or your project's location.

2. **C**   Do you want to invest in stocks, shares, bonds and currencies around the world? + We specialise in the US, UK, China, Australia and Canada markets, but we have opportunities from all around the world.

3. **B**   We have hundreds of genuine, satisfied customers who you can contact to hear about our professional service.

4. **C**   Check us out today on our website and book an online or call-back consultation with one of our investment executives.

5. **B**   Call Howard Solicitors for our no win no fee service.

6. **A**   Flexible payment options with installments

7. **D**   Commercial & Residential, Construction, Barn Conversions, Alterations & Extensions + Building Defect Analysis

8. **FALSE**   Bournepoint is one of the largest shopping parks in the country

9. **TRUE**   Next year, the CinePlus Multiplex Cinema will open

10. **NOT GIVEN**   There is nothing in the text relating to this and so the answer is 'not given' in the text.

11. **TRUE**   The bowling is very popular at weekend evenings, so booking this in advance is a good idea.

12. **FALSE**   There are photocopying, printing, Internet, fax and national telephone services available as part of the price.

13. **TRUE**   Large D locks are easier to use and can lock several bikes at a time, but mini D locks are light and easy to carry, plus they are harder for thieves to break.

14. **NOT GIVEN**   There is nothing in the text relating to this and so the answer is 'not given' in the text.

15. **tailored**   When you join Dawson's, we will create a personal development plan for you. In consultation with you, we will identify your strengths and weaknesses, and take into account the way you like to learn.

16. **skills**   *you* choose what new abilities you feel you need to improve working for us.

17. **resign**   we demonstrate to our workforce that we value you enough to invest in you; this can improve staff retention.

18. **assessment**   employees must pay us back if they don't complete or pass the course (if evaluation is part of the course)

19. **relevance**   Be careful to include the dates, training fees, any travel or accommodation expenses and how the training applies to you and your role at Dawson's.

20. **in-house**   Some of these courses are run by specialists who are already part of our company and others are outsourced to organisations that specialise in the relevant field.

21. **morale**   In addition to all this, a green office can have a significant effect on employees in terms of morale. + Adding a green aspect to the office equation can also help to make members of a team more aware of their actions with regard to the environment, which is fantastic; it may also add to their work ethic as well.

22. **Shortcomings**   Paying closer attention to details in one aspect of life can lead to recognising shortcomings in others.

23. **recycling facility**   Contact a nearby recycling facility and establish what materials they accept.

24. **regulations**   For businesses, there may be regulations on the disposal of electronics, batteries and mercury-containing lamps, as they may contain hazardous substances.

25. **leftovers**   After office festivities, put leftovers in recyclable containers, and share them with family, friends, or others.

26. **durability**   Consider the durability of a product before you purchase it.

27. **symbiosis**   Green offices connect the business aspect of life to the natural world, which in turn can help to create a symbiosis between the two.

28. **scientific research**   The possibility of a different type of life, in imaginable or unimaginable forms, has shaped scientific research and the development of different cultures and traditions around the world.

29. **waterways**   Astronomer Schiaparelli's observations two hundred and seventy years later resulted in a superficial map of Mars' surface being constructed, containing linear features. These, Schiaparelli said, hinted at waterways, possibly created by an intelligent race.

30. **uninhabitable**   the hope of another form of life on Mars was not completely given up until the 1960's, when NASA's Mariner spacecraft landed on Mars and finally provided photographs and scientific evidence that gave proof of the uninhabitable nature of Earth's red neighbour.

31. **samples**   A study released recently reports that ancient Mars harboured a form of nitrogen that could potentially have been used by microbes, if any existed, to build key molecules, such as amino acids. Bored samples from a sedimentary mudstone had previously allowed Mars-rover team members to conclude that, billions of years ago, the area was part of a potentially life-supporting lake-and-stream system.

32. **controversial**   Today, different projects and organisations have tried to shed light on the controversial issue of intelligent life in outer space.

33. **distances**   Even though this does not eliminate the possibility of other forms of life, it does imply that if they do exist, they do so far from our reach, and these distances complicate any advances in the field.

34. **lasers**   It is likely that lasers will be developed to exploit their even greater range within a few years.

35. **range**   It is likely that lasers will be developed to exploit their even greater range within a few years.

36. **FALSE**   The "Wow Signal" is regarded as being an exception. It was a signal picked up by a telescope at an American university in 1977 and appeared to have all the right characteristics to have originated from an intelligent species. The fact that no signal was ever received from the same area of the sky again led to the event being regarded as a coincidence or a misinterpretation.

37. **FALSE**   The opinion that this may bring a threat to mankind's existence is not as abstract as it has been presented in many science fiction movies, and scientists as well as astronomers are reluctant to pursue active signalling.

38. **NOT GIVEN**   There is nothing in the text relating to this and so the answer is 'not given' in the text.

39. **D**   Thirdly, and most importantly though, they would need to exist in the same era as us.

40. **C**   However, due to the fact that the development from one-celled organisms to several-celled ones is very unlikely and the emergence of intelligence is even more unlikely, many renowned scientists are now less optimistic and are convinced that, at present, we are the only intelligent species in this galaxy.

GENERAL READING TEST 12

1. **anxiety**   The most difficult time is waiting for the surgery. If possible, having someone to sit with you before it takes place - perhaps a relative or a friend - may help to diminish anxiety.

2. **email**   At some hospitals, you'll be asked to attend a pre-operative assessment, which may be an appointment with a nurse or doctor, a telephone assessment or an email assessment.

3. **blood**   If the assessment involves a visit to the hospital, some tests may be carried out, including a blood test.

4. **medications**   You'll be given clear information on the following: ... whether you should cease taking your usual medications before going into hospital

5. **anaesthetic**   If your doctor has instructed you to fast before the operation, it's really important that you don't eat or drink anything – this includes light snacks, sweets and water. You need an empty stomach during surgery, so you don't vomit while you're under anaesthetic.

6. **blood circulation**   You'll need to remove all make-up and nail polish before your operation, as the hospital staff will need to see your skin and nails to make sure your blood circulation is healthy.

7. **checklist**   There is so much to organise in just packing for the move that important things are often over-looked. Take advantage of a checklist to make sure you've got everything covered.

8. **council tax**   Contact your local rates office to let them know the date you move out of your current property and when you move into your new one, so they bill you correctly for council tax.

9. **redirect**   To deal with this, redirect your mail to your new address. You can download a form from the Post Office website. It can take up to 10 days to set up and there is a charge.

10. **meters**   On your moving day, you will need to read the meters in both dwellings, so the right bills can be issued.

11. **window**   Any spare keys should be clearly labeled and left where they will be seen when you leave the house on moving day. Don't leave them in direct view of any window.

12. **TRUE**   Sections of the East High Street will be closed from Monday, April 6, for up to 12 weeks to allow for Campion Gas to replace and reinforce gas networks. Your local council is taking the closure as an opportunity to carry out street lighting improvements at the same time so as to minimise possible future disruption.

13. **NOT GIVEN**   There is nothing in the text relating to this and so the answer is 'not given' in the text.

14. **FALSE**   One lane only on South Street will also be closed.

15. **The staff management**   For us, the main issue is the staff management of those who work on their own and away from the main business base.

16. **loneliness**   For you, it can include overcoming loneliness

17. **Promotion**   Often, being away from the managers who are responsible for promotion is felt to be the greatest disadvantage.

18. **The employee's post**   Homeworking can also be used in conjunction with other arrangements, such as flexible hours, working part-time, term-time working or working our core hours. The employee's post will determine whether this is possible.

19. **A risk assessment**   As the employer of all our staff, we have a duty of care for all our employees, and the requirements of the health and safety legislation apply to homeworkers. We are responsible for carrying out a risk assessment

20. **Overhead house lighting**   For example, even with great natural light in people's home offices, you'll still need additional lighting for darker hours of the day, as overhead house lighting is usually insufficient for work.

21. **prevention**   Don't wait for it to make you ill before you do something about it.

22. **bed**   You may feel like lying down, but this won't help and could make things worse.

23. **technique**   Incorrect procedure when using a computer keyboard and mouse, mobile phone or hand-held device can all cause RSI.

24. **breaks**   If you work on a computer a lot, it's important to leave the computer periodically. That means for every hour at your keyboard, you should rest for at least five to ten minutes.

25. **commute**   Many of us spend long hours at work and may have long and tiring journeys to and from work.

26. **fitness**   But getting active at work is easier than you may think. Try and cycle or walk to work, take stairs rather than the lift or use your lunch break as an exercise slot. Working out and losing weight will also benefit your posture and help prevent injury.

27. **performance**   What we eat and drink affects not just our health, but our efficiency and success too.

28. **ix**   Various information within Paragraph A.

29. **iv**   Various information within Paragraph B.

30. **v**   Various information within Paragraph C.

31. **ii**   Various information within Paragraph D.

32. **viii**   Various information within Paragraph E.

33. **vi**   Various information within Paragraph F.

34. **x**   Various information within Paragraph G.

35. **B*** Rocky terrain and difficult weather conditions made the task appear impossible and the bridge's detractors publicised this.

36. **C*** Aesthetes and environmentalists worried the bridge would mar the natural attractiveness of San Francisco's world-famed harbour.

37. **E*** A series of other accusations followed: an enemy fleet could demolish the bridge and bottle-up the US fleet.

38. **G*** The floor of the Golden Gate Strait would not support the load of the bridge.

39. **H*** Voters, despite the financial insecurity that was used as further grounds to oppose the bridge.

40. **C** This is a holistic answer and involves synthesis of the whole text. This text in its entirety fits "To provide an overview of the construction and use of the Golden Gate Bridge." better than the other three answers.

GENERAL READING TEST 13

1. **E**   ($60 call-out charge)

2. **B**   References available.

3. **C**   Contact me at sally@online.com.au.

4. **H**   All payments to be done by credit or debit card at the time of ordering.

5. **D**   I do all types of housework, and I can also handle your laundry, washing up or childcare.

6. **C**   I charge $10 an hour and I ask for a taxi to take me home if I stay at your home after 11 p.m.

7. **D**   I do all types of housework, and I can also handle your laundry

8. **H**   Call or use our website to place your orders.

9. **The head waiter**   Ask the head waiter which sitting you have been allocated. She can change this if space is available.

10. **A small deposit**   All sun loungers and tables on the beach are free of charge for our residents, but a small deposit is required.

11. **The nurse** For anything more serious or problems in the hotel, there is the nurse on duty 24/7 in the hotel

12. **Hotel residents**   The main hotel swimming pool area is also solely accessible by hotel residents.

13. **In plastic receptacles**   Please note that all drinks will be supplied in plastic receptacles, as glass can be a potential danger by the pool.

14. **(The) entertainment board**   Check the entertainment board for the weekly plan.

15. **notice**   it would be best to do this in writing giving the correct amount of notice.

16. **pay**   You're usually due the normal pay and things like sick leave before you leave.

17. **issues**   Although you don't need to give details at this point, it might be a good idea to let your company know if there are any outstanding issues you're dealing with that might be affected by your leaving.

18. **counter offer**   The most likely way an employer will try and make you stay is by proposing a pay rise either equal to or above what you've been offered in your new job and/or by suggesting promotion and/or added benefits. Make sure you understand the counter offer and avoid making a knee jerk decision.

19. **in lieu**   Once you resign, your employer can ask you to leave immediately. In this case they'll probably offer you a one-off payment in lieu, instead of allowing you to work out your time.

20. **reference**   Try and leave your job on a suitable footing with people. Firstly, any new employer may want a reference from your old employer.

21. **responsibilities**   Don't expect everyone to be glad about your leaving. Some people might take it personally and it might mean that some of your co-workers have to take on the responsibilities that you are leaving.

22. **F**   Punctuality is always a difficult thing for managers to enforce, as there are often reasons for lateness. No supervisor likes to be heavy-handed and antagonise people. + The policy will therefore help support the supervisors as well as make things clear for all employees.

23. **B**   The late employee cannot complete tasks, is not there to take part in teams and will need to be covered by colleagues, which stops the colleagues from fulfilling their own responsibilities.

24. **I**   This can be very demotivating for the late workers' colleagues, when they see people getting away with unprofessional conduct.

25. **G**   Next week at 10 a.m., we will be holding a mandatory meeting for all staff, where the draft policy will be discussed. All employees will be allowed to ask questions and make their points of view known.

26. **C**   After next week's meeting, a draft punctuality policy will be drawn up by the Human Resources Department. The draft will be first reviewed by senior management, who will recommend changes as they see fit. When the next draft is ready, the policy will be shared with all employees and everyone will be given the chance to give feedback and voice concerns. After all the feedback has been collected and assessed, the final policy will be published.

27. **A**   When the policy is ready, all employees will be asked to add their signature to it to show they have read and understood everything in it. Following this, the policy will be put into action straight away, so no employee will be able to continue with this counter-productive behaviour.

28. **TRUE**   The dingo's origin is uncertain

29. **NOT GIVEN**   There is nothing in the text relating to this and so the answer is 'not given' in the text.

30. **TRUE**   However, dingo populations multiplied and evidence has shown that they began to thrive on the newly imported European rabbits that were running in feral plagues at the same time.

31. **TRUE**   Bounties have been placed on the heads of dingoes in southeastern Australia since as early as 1852. While bounties were placed on numerous types of animals, the bounties given for dingoes were generally the highest and often twice as much was given for a dingo than for other pests, such as foxes, hares, and wallabies.

32. **FALSE**   As time went on, neighbouring livestock properties grouped together to become enclosed within vermin-proof fences.

33. **C**   Over time, the length of the fence has also been reduced within Queensland for cost reasons and control over the dingo population is often done via less expensive poisoning, specifically via bait laced with sodium monofluoroacetate.

34. **D**   Feral camels are also smashing through sections of the fence in search of water and recommendations to reinforce and electrify more portions of the fence have been made to deal with this.

35. **C**   The Dog Fence Act 1946 levied a rate on grazing properties located inside the fence to fund wages for maintenance and patrol workers.

36. **B**   The sloping dog fence is recommended for most locations, except in situations where the soil is susceptible to erosion, as this may result in the formation of gaps below the fence.

37. **A**   The fence's low electric wires are also likely to be problematic in environments with considerable ground vegetation, which will cause electrical shorts and leakage.

38. **timber posts**   Every section of the fence is just over a metre high and has six wires, consecutively electrically charged and earthed, that go between timber posts down from the top until around 30 centimetres from the bottom.

39. **earthed**   The wires then slope out to the ground at approximately a 30-degree angle with four more wires, again consecutively electrically charged and earthed.

40. **more narrowly spaced**   The lower wires then angle out to the ground at approximately a 30-degree angle with four more wires, again consecutively electrically charged and earthed. These angled bottom wires are more narrowly spaced, as this is where pressure from dingoes is greatest.

GENERAL READING TEST 14

1. **The town Mayor**   The day will start at 11 a.m., when the town Mayor will formally launch the anniversary celebration with a short speech in the town gardens.

2. **9 p.m.**   All the town centre's shops will be open and their normal closing time of 7 p.m. will be extended to 9 p.m., so the shopaholics amongst you can have the time of your lives.

3. **The Children's Hospital**   If there is any excess revenue left at the end of the day, the money will ALL go to the Children's Hospital.

4. **Various bands**   There will be various bands playing and everyone should find something to their taste.

5. **A firework display** At 10 p.m., there will be a firework display to end the day's fun.

6. **by night bus**   People will be able to get back to their respective suburbs by night bus, and plenty of these will be laid on for free from 11 p.m. for one hour.

7. **Special constables**   Special constables will be on hand to watch over everything, but we hope that they won't be needed.

8. **TRUE**   You must be at least 16 years old before you can apply for your learner licence and you first have to pass a road theory exam before you can get it.

9. **NOT GIVEN**   There is nothing in the text relating to this and so the answer is 'not given' in the text.

10. **FALSE**   To apply for your restricted licence, you must be at least 16½ years old and have held your learner licence for at least six months.

11. **TRUE**   You can drive on your own, but not between 10 p.m. and 5 a.m.

12. **FALSE**   Your supervisor must hold a current full New Zealand car licence that does not have a supervisor condition. They must have held their full New Zealand licence (or an equivalent overseas licence) for at least two years.

13. **FALSE**   You must be at least 18 years of age before you can apply for your full licence. If you have completed an approved advanced driving skills course, this is reduced to 17½.

14. **NOT GIVEN**   There is nothing in the text relating to this and so the answer is 'not given' in the text.

15. **self-employed**   These notes are meant to help any agency workers who are assigned to us. We hope that you enjoy your time with us and that it is profitable for both you and the company. These notes do not cover people who are self-employed.

16. **personnel department**   On their first day, all agency workers should report by 8 a.m. to Mr. Buckley, who is to be found in the personnel department.

17. **break times**   When you get to your department, your department manager will tell you about your duties. The working day finishes at 5 p.m. All agency workers are allowed an hour for their lunch break and they are also entitled to morning and afternoon breaks. Your department manager will tell you the break times in your department.

18. **job vacancies**   From day one of their employment, any agency worker will be entitled to: + be informed about any job vacancies.

19. **responsibility**   Your 12 weeks will start again if you get a new job at a different workplace, have a break of more than 6 weeks between jobs at Greening Ltd., or stay at Greening Ltd. but take a new role that has more substantial responsibility.

20. **Ante-natal appointments**   All agency workers, regardless of how long they have been with Greening Ltd., will also be entitled to paid time off to go to ante-natal appointments during their working hours.

21. **trade union representative**   All agency workers are welcome to talk with the trade union representative (Mrs. White in the post room on the 4th floor) with regard to their rights and obligations.

22. **flexibility**   Renting can firstly provide more flexibility for your business as it grows.

23. **lease**   You are not locked into property ownership and you can usually agree with your landlord the length of the lease that you require, or have a break clause included.

24. **deposit**   Upfront charges for leasing premises are often relatively low, though you will have to provide a deposit.

25. **interest rate**   You are not exposed to interest rate rises, although your rent may rise periodically as a result of rent reviews.

26. **risk assessment**   You must perform a risk assessment in the workplace and take steps to remove any hazards and potential risks.

27. **rental contract**   The advantage to a renter is that the landlord should pay for all or at least a part of any improvements that you feel will improve the energy performance of the building. These responsibilities though should be laid out in your rental contract.

28. **iv**   Various information within Paragraph A.

29. **vi**   Various information within Paragraph B.

30. **ix**   Various information within Paragraph C.

31. **i**   Various information within Paragraph D.

32. **viii**   Various information within Paragraph E.

33. **iii**   Various information within Paragraph F.

34. **C**   Drowning claims an estimated 372,000 lives around the world each year. This is a conservative estimate and the actual number is likely to be much higher.

35. **G**   In the early 19th century, there was an average of 1800 shipwrecks a year around the coasts of Great Britain, with many sailors drowned. This danger was a tolerated part of life onboard.

36. **E**   One of the entries, from William Wouldhave, was designed to self right. Boatbuilder Henry Greathead was asked to build a lifeboat combining the best features of Lukin's and Wouldhave's plans, and came up with a vessel called the Original.

37. **B**   Sir William Hillary is credited with founding the RNLI. After witnessing the destruction of dozens of ships from his home on the Isle of Man, and getting involved in rescue attempts himself, Hillary appealed to the Navy, the government and other 'eminent characters' for help in forming 'a national institution for the preservation of lives and property from shipwreck'.

38. **C**   Efforts in the mid 19th century were focused on the wealthy, and it wasn't until the late 1880's that the RNLI realised how generous the general public could be.

39. **B**   Lifeboats were frequently dragged for long distances before putting to sea to minimise the time at sea in rough conditions.

40. **C**   The way in which the public uses the sea has changed dramatically since the RNLI's foundation. More individuals are using the water for leisure, so the lifesaving service has had to change accordingly.

GENERAL READING TEST 15

1. **(sample) work**   Prospective parents and students will be able to find all the information they want from those on duty and they'll also be able to examine sample work studied by all the years studying at the school.

2. **head of marketing**   At 11 a.m., there will be a short talk by our head of marketing and this will be followed by a short questions – answers session.

3. **website**   DO look over our website first, so that you don't ask unnecessary questions

4. **primary school**   DO tell your primary school that you and your child are attending our Open Day

5. **feedback**   DO provide us with feedback on the day, so we can make it better next year

6. **morning**   DON'T come too late – the morning is always the most useful time

7. **noise**   DON'T make too much noise in class time

8. **B**   Personalise your letter. While it's a temptation to use one letter for all applications when you're filling in a lot, a letter tailored to the job on offer is much more likely to make a positive impact on the employer.

9. **H**   Target the skills required for the job and show how your experience, qualifications and personal qualities make you a match for it. Emphasise any job-appropriate education or course certificates you have.

10. **K**   Be formal. Of course it's important to have friendly staff, but people expect high formality in job applications. It's the same for an interview.

11. **A**   Use a computer to write your covering letter. This is what will be expected and, while a hand-written letter may seem more personal, it will seem strange nowadays.

12. **D**   The letter should also be checked for grammar and spelling errors, and should use the same text format and font size throughout.

13. **F**   Call the company and find who will be reading it and direct it to him/her.

14. **J**   If you're sending the application by electronic mail, don't forget to attach your covering letter and CV.

15. **Forward-rotating programs**   Forward-rotating programs (moving from morning to afternoon to night shifts) are better than backward-rotating ones in terms of sleep loss and tiredness.

16. **8 hours**   To qualify as night working, the night time period must be no more than 8 hours long

Page 134

17. **The action report**   The latest risk assessment and the action report on work to address any issues is always available.

18. **The company secretary**   Please ask the company secretary before lunch on the day of travel, so that you can get an assured booking.

19. **The self-employed**   Our usual limits and regulations for night workers do not apply to the self-employed working with us.

20. **Health professionals**   we must perform a health assessment before you become a night worker and on a regular basis after that. Usually, this is just done with a series of questions, which was created in collaboration with health professionals.

21. **TRUE**   In most situations, small investments of time and money can achieve large improvements in information security.

22. **NOT GIVEN**   There is nothing in the text relating to this and so the answer is 'not given' in the text.

23. **TRUE**   ranging from the accidental loss of data to deliberate sabotage by staff (though the latter is very rare).

24. **FALSE**   Best practice for backing up data includes: + giving one person the main duty for backing up, and designating a second to cover for absence

25. **FALSE**   Best practice for backing up data includes: + not relying solely on a cloud-based backup system for keeping your data safe

26. **TRUE**   Best practice for backing up data includes: + using a different tape, external hard drive or disk to back up each day of the week and having a schedule for rotating them – this can nearly always safeguard backups in the case of a malware attack or the like

27. **NOT GIVEN**   There is nothing in the text relating to this and so the answer is 'not given' in the text.

28. **AC**   Alan Cook, explains. "It is not known whether the population is properly recovering. There is a real concern that the drastically depleted genetic pool created by the hunting will affect their capacity to breed properly. Only time will tell if the figures continue to grow."

29. **SM**   Scientist, Sophie Morton, explains how whale experts try and work out their age. "We have discovered that by counting the layers of a deceased whale's wax-like earplugs, we can get a close estimate of the animal's age. The oldest blue whale found using this method was determined to be around 110 years old and we estimate that average lifespan is estimated at around 80 to 90 years."

30. **PL**   Conservationist Patrick Liley explains why the blue whale fat is one factor that has threatened the blue whale. "Historically, hunters have chased them to harvest their meat and render the cold-resistant fat down to oil.

31. **MD**   Dr Mike Dance, said, "Using innovative advanced echosounders, we were able to track individual krill for the first time, allowing an examination of the changing internal structure of the krill swarms that blue whales prey upon. Our ability to find these blue whales also allowed us to investigate the whales' habitat."

32. **AS**   Marine biologist, Ariadne Scott, describes them. "An average individual is 21 metres long and weighs 100 tons. It has almost 2,500 gallons of blood and burns up to 3 million calories a day. Its heart weighs more than a ton and the tongue alone weighs about 2 tons."

33. **PL**   Patrick Liley explains what he feels is the solution. "It's not a secret. Whaling caused the initial destruction of the blue whale, and it continues to do so. We need to make all countries stop whaling and close the loophole on 'whaling for scientific purposes' that permits commercial whaling to carry on."

34. **JS**   Jon Stephens explains, things change in winter. "Summers are spent in polar waters, because food production is higher there, but in winter, they migrate several thousand miles to warmer tropic and subtropic areas and fast for the duration of their stay while breeding, using the fat on their bodies to see them through the whole winter."

35. **AB**   Alice Baggley, an environment spokesperson, explains the problem. "There is concern that noise pollution may affect blue whales' ability to communicate, particularly in New Zealand, where there is persistent seismic activity for oil and gas extraction near a blue whale foraging ground."

36. **B**   Blue whales are also the loudest animals on Earth, with their calls reaching 188 decibels (a jet reaches 140 decibels). Recently, Australian marine scientists have detected individuals singing from almost 750 kilometres away. Although no one is certain, the blue whale calls are theorised to be probably a part of breeding behaviour.

37. **D**   Blue whales usually only congregate for this reproduction and they do not live in the pods common for other whale species.

38. **A**   The blue whale is currently one of the world's most endangered whales. It was not hunted until modern techniques made them more easily attainable, but by the mid-1900's, only about 1,000 were estimated to remain.

39. **B**   Blue whales have been protected from whaling since 1966 by the International Whaling Commission, though some were hunted unlawfully until 1972.

40. **C**   Like many marine animals, blue whales are at risk of 'bycatch', which is accidental entanglement in fishing gear, which can cause injury, infections, starvation and drowning.

EXAMPLE WRITING ANSWERS

Below you will find example writing answers for all the writing questions in the General Practice Tests 11 to 15. There are many ways of answering the writing questions and these examples are only one possibility of a good answer. Please refer to the question papers while you are reading these letters and essays so that you understand the questions that are being answered. We hope this will give you an insight into how the writing answers should be written for IELTS General module in order to get a Band 8 - 8.5.

GENERAL WRITING PRACTICE TEST 11

Task 1

Dear Jimmy,

Guess what! I have finally moved into my new house! The furniture is already arranged and the boxes that you saw at my old apartment last time containing all the decorations have disappeared.

I would love you to come over for a few weeks to stay. I would appreciate your company and we can finish off any last adjustments together. I know that you are creative and so maybe you have some tips for me on how to decorate the living room. Besides a huge bookshelf, a TV and a sofa, I am unsure about what else to put in there. What do you think about next Friday? You can come anytime, but this would be most convenient for me.

I am sure that you will like my new house, just as I do. The garden has exquisite flowers and herbs from its previous owners and the large stove in the kitchen gives you a feeling of nostalgia. In addition to this, the staircase creaks in a funny way, which reminds me of the old house where I lived in as a child.

I am looking forward to your answer and I hope that you can come as soon as possible!

Hugs,

Leah

(205 words)

Task 2

In modern day society, it is essential for a child to be educated in order for him or her to have success later on in life. Children are typically educated in schools, which are run by the government. The government officials therefore decide what is taught to the children and what is not. Personally, I believe that it is better if governments are responsible for the subject matter covered in school and not the teachers.

It is a common goal to supply all children with the same opportunities in life, meaning that the same core knowledge should be taught to all children to offer them the same benefits. Naturally, some children will be better at certain subjects than others and will therefore obtain a more detailed degree of knowledge, yet every child should be taught the same core knowledge. Education provides opportunities, because certain types of education will enable children to pursue certain careers later on in life.

Supplying the same core knowledge is an essential concept, yet it has not been put into action in several countries. In Germany, for example, the syllabus taught depends on the region of the country. In certain regions, children attend school for thirteen years and in other regions for twelve years. This raises the question whether or not the children obtain the same degree of knowledge and that the children attending school for thirteen years are at an advantage compared to those attending school for twelve years. Already one can see that problems arise when the regional government decides upon the core knowledge taught to students. If teachers had a say in what knowledge should be taught to students, the subject matter would become even more complex. The core knowledge would not only vary from region to region, yet also from school to school, providing unfair advantages and disadvantages for certain students.

In conclusion, the government of a country should decide upon what knowledge is taught in schools, as the situation would become too complex if all teachers were responsible for this aspect.

(339 words)

GENERAL WRITING PRACTICE TEST 12

Task 1

Dear Sir / Madam,

I am a student at Mason College and I would like to enquire about the event hall that you own in the city centre.

My friends and I are trying to establish a weekly dance club session and have been on the lookout for a suitable location. The dance club will be focused on Charleston and Rock'n'Roll dancing, which are becoming increasingly popular at our college. Having inquired at the city's town hall, I have been given your contact information and would like to ask whether it is possible to rent your hall and what the conditions would be for this. We would need the hall every Tuesday from 6:30 p.m. to 8:30 p.m. During public holidays and college semester breaks, the hall will not be needed. I would be happy to meet you at the hall one evening after my classes to discuss the possibility of this rental.

I hope to hear back from you soon with a positive reply.

Yours sincerely,

Paulho Gomez   *(169 words)*

Task 2

Illegal drugs have become a worldwide problem in modern day society. The trading of drugs is widespread in nearly all countries and the number of people consuming drugs worldwide is high. It has been suggested simply to legalise all recreational drugs to solve the problems associated with them. I personally agree partially with this proposal, because I can see many advantages, yet also many disadvantages.

One positive aspect of legalising these drugs would be that the number of criminal activities committed to obtain them would decrease. Fewer people would therefore be imprisoned and have a criminal history that prevents them from progressing in life. Additionally, essential police resources would be freed up and devoted to other areas. Finally, high taxes could be imposed on the legal product, allowing governments to have better resources to improve the infrastructure of their countries.

Although legalising all illegal drugs could result in several positive effects, there are many negative effects that could be possible. As a result of the legalisation, I personally believe that it would become acceptable to use drugs and people would no longer pay attention to the damage that drugs cause. Schools might no longer educate teenagers and adolescents about the negative effects drugs have on people, resulting in more teenagers experimenting with them, as they would believe that this is a normal aspect of life. This would result in a higher number of drug addicts and potentially in more deaths, because it would be easier to obtain a large amount of illegal drugs and therefore the chances of overdosing would also increase.

In conclusion, I partially agree with the proposed action. Nonetheless, I think that an age restriction should be placed on drug use, as teenagers and adolescents could easily become addicted if all illegal drugs are legalised. This group of people is highly at risk of becoming addicted and potentially dying as a result of drug use and therefore should only be allowed to consume drugs after reaching a certain age.

GENERAL WRITING PRACTICE TEST 13

Task 1

Dear Tom,

I have rather upsetting news for you, for which I am very sorry. Although my stay with you in two weeks has been planned for a while, I will have to cancel.

Yesterday during work, I had another meeting with a colleague regarding the town hall project, which I told you about the past few months. During the conversation, a business trip, which had been planned and booked since last year, came up. I will need to speak to several representatives of other town halls in the area. I had completely forgotten about this, and unfortunately it is at the exact same time as my planned stay at your house. I hope you won't be too angry with me, I hope to make it up to you in some other way.

Why don't I come and visit you at the end of your vacation, when you have returned from Europe? I remember you saying that you have three weeks left before going to New York. If that works for you, please get back to me, as I would love to see you before Christmas.

Hope to see you soon!

Best wishes,

Johnny

(194 words)

Task 2

In modern day society, money is a driving force for nearly everyone. Most people aspire to have lots of money and to have the ability to live the life they want. In order to obtain money, people work in different jobs. In some countries around the world, governments have initiated a system where unemployed people receive a regular payment to enable them to survive. This system is often controversial. Some people believe it is an excellent idea, whilst others believe that it puts an unreasonable strain on a country's financial resources.

When looking at the positive aspects of this system, it can be said that it prevents people from having a private bankruptcy. When somebody becomes unemployed, he or she will have on-going costs such as rent for a dwelling, bills for water, telephone and electricity as well as the cost of food and several other things. Without a salary, this person will fall into debt, because they will be unable to cover these costs. A national unemployment payment system will therefore prevent this person from losing nearly everything over time. Without this system, many people would become homeless and would potentially engage in criminal activities to survive. Therefore, one can say that this system is positive. Although stories are heard of people exploiting the system, usually people that become unemployed want to find new employment fast in order to become financially independent again, meaning that the government does not have to pay a regular payment for long.

Although there are positive aspects of this system, one can also say that if the payment made by the government is too high, it will prevent people from seeking for work actively. Occasionally, the payment people receive is higher than their potential salaries, deterring them from working and creating an on-going cost for the government.

In conclusion, the proposed system has positive and negative aspects. Personally, I believe that the positive effects of the system outweigh the negative. The payment must remain on a level that helps people survive without regular salaries, but does not seem attractive to exploit over a longer period of time.

(353 words)

GENERAL WRITING PRACTICE TEST 14

Task 1

Dear Mr. and Mrs. Greene,

My name is Caroline Hague and I am an exchange student about to participate in an English Language Training course in London. The organisation that arranged this course for me has assigned you to be my host family for those four weeks and I would therefore like to introduce myself.

I come from the Netherlands and live in Maastricht, a beautiful and historical city not too far away from the country's capital, Amsterdam. I would like to know more about the English language, culture and literature and therefore I have applied for this training course. I am an active outdoor person and love to ride my bike, and I am also passionate about music.

I am interested in the type of food that is popular in your family, as I am a vegetarian. Do you eat a lot of meat? If yes, that's no problem for me, I will only have to know in advance so I can bring a few essentials.

In a month's time, on the twenty-second of May, I will be arriving at Gatwick airport at 4 p.m. I have seen that you have kindly offered to pick me up and so I will be waiting at the Terminal A pick-up at 5.15 p.m. I look forward to meeting you then.

I hope to hear back from you and to see you soon!

Regards,

Caroline Hague

(234 words)

Task 2

Students today have many possibilities when it comes to choosing a possible career, however, their choice often involves the decision of whether or not they would like to go to university to study a certain subject in depth or if they would like to go directly into the workplace. This decision should be entirely dependent on the student.

It is generally thought that students who go directly into the workplace after leaving school are less intelligent than those who study further on at university. Although this stereotype might be true in some cases, it often is not. In the case that a student wants to have a job such as optician, he or she does not need to study at university and can go directly into workplace to learn how to carry out this job. This student will have to pass certain exams, which are just as important as the exams taken at university, in order to obtain a licence for carrying out this profession. Going directly into workplace therefore similarly involves studying and learning like at university. Students who wish to pursue a career such as doctor or lawyer will have to go to university to learn more about this profession. Once they have passed all necessary exams, they will be ready to enter the profession.

Naturally a certain degree of intelligence is necessary to attend university and therefore for students who did not obtain an adequate education it will not be possible to attend university. Although this might seem unjust, students with low intelligence or students who have not been well educated will only hinder other students in the learning process.

In conclusion, I personally think that it should be up to the student whether he or she would like to go directly into the workplace or study further at university. The student must be happy with the choice he or she made and should choose the option suitable for making them happy in the future.

(328 words)

GENERAL WRITING PRACTICE TEST 15

Task 1

Dear Roy,

I am participating in a theatre event at college next week and have been designated the photographer's role. I know that you have a single-lens reflex camera of very good quality and would like to ask you if I may borrow it for this event.

The event is next Saturday and Sunday, as there are two performances, and I will be sitting in the audience and going around to get close-ups of the actors. I would need the camera from 6 p.m. to 9 p.m. on Saturday and Sunday. If you are willing to leave the camera with me overnight, that would be easier. I promise to take good care of it and lock it away as soon as I am otherwise engaged. I can return the camera to you either on Sunday evening or Monday morning, depending on what suits you best.

Please tell me as soon as possible if you are willing to lend me your camera, as I need to tell my teachers if I will be taking part in the event.

Regards,

Bill

(178 words)

Task 2

In recent years, computer use around the world has increased drastically. As a result technological equipment is used increasingly in schools around the world. Many people question therefore whether schools put enough emphasis on teaching students basic handwriting skills and mental mathematic skills.

The use of technological equipment in lessons has increased since the onset of the digital age. Nearly all professions around the world involve computer use and even the simplest tasks are carried out via electronic equipment. It is therefore important for students to learn how to use technological equipment correctly for their future careers. This equipment also offers various learning advantages, as notes and assignments can be completed much faster and more neatly using electronic equipment.

Nonetheless, the practical skills such as using and holding a pen correctly are likewise vital for future careers. Students therefore have to be taught at early ages how to carry out simple tasks using basic skills, such as writing. It is also essential that a student develops neat handwriting, as in the case of a technological problem the student will have to write by hand. Furthermore, final exams are typically written by hand and thus the student must develop the basic skill of holding a pen and writing with it. It is the same with mathematics skills. People will not always have a machine with them to carry out calculations and the ability to do arithmetic in the head is a vital skill for operating in today's world.

In conclusion, I personally believe that schools should keep a balance between using practical skills and using electronic equipment to carry out certain tasks by having student submit assignments created electronically, yet also by having them complete assignments by hand in class and without computers or calculators. This balance is important, as if the focus lies only on one of the two aspects, the student will face problems later on in life.

(321 words)

COMMENTARY ON THE EXAMPLE SPEAKING RECORDINGS

In this section you will find reports by an IELTS speaking examiner on the recordings of **Speaking Tests 11 - 15**. The questions asked in the recordings are the questions in the Speaking Tests 11 – 15, so, while listening to the recordings, it is advised to have the questions with you for reference. The recordings are not real IELTS test recordings, but the interviewer is a real IELTS examiner and the recordings are conducted in the exact way that an IELTS Speaking Test is done.

SPEAKING PRACTICE TEST 11

Examiner's Commentary

The person interviewed is Pedro, a Chilean male. Pedro is a teacher.

Part 1

Pedro spoke very fluently and accurately. He has a very slight accent, but his accent often seems to be more American than Chilean. He spoke calmly, and with humour and intelligence. Pedro's vocabulary range is very strong and he rarely needs to pause to access the right word. There were very few errors, though there were occasional inconsistencies ("it's played along the year" instead of 'all through the year')

Part 2

Pedro had no problems with speaking for the longer Part 2. He again spoke fluently and accurately with his negligible Chilean accent. His vocabulary range was extremely good, with no apparent problems.

Part 3

Pedro again gave measured and full answers. He was accurate, fluent and clear. His pronunciation was again very good, with his American accent clearly apparent. He did use some slightly different intonation, which made some words sound a little different to how a native speaker would pronounce them. There were no particular grammar or word choice problems.

Marking - The marking of the IELTS Speaking Test is done in 4 parts.

Fluency and Coherence	9
Lexical Resource	9
Grammatical Range and Accuracy	9
Pronunciation	8

Estimated IELTS Speaking Band   **8.5**

SPEAKING PRACTICE TEST 12

Examiner's Commentary

The person interviewed is Kuba, a Polish male. Kuba is a professional diver.

Part 1

Kuba spoke fairly fluently and generally accurately. Kuba had a good answer for all the questions, but there were certain limitations in his vocabulary and grammar range and he often had to pause to access language and sometimes tailed off. This led to fairly short answers for some of the questions. Quite often though, Kuba did show that he knew some more unusual lexis, probably due to the time that he spent in the US, which he mentioned in Part 2. Kuba's accent was quite strong, but did not really affect communication.

Part 2

Kuba spoke well and confidently in this Part. He still had some limitations in vocabulary and grammar and he also made occasional errors (i.e. "I used to work as a card dealer in casino" instead of "I used to work as a card dealer in a casino"). This error was typical for him, as he made quite a few article errors, which often happens with Slavic languages. Kuba lacked a little fluency in places and at one time he had to stop, as he could not access the word "environment" (a word he remembered just after the test stopped).

Part 3

The more demanding nature of the questions in Part 3 led to Kuba making shorter and sometimes less fluent answers here, although he also gave some good and long answers. The grammar and vocabulary range were reasonable, but again there was a lack of range that showed Kuba's limitations.

Marking - The marking of the IELTS Speaking Test is done in 4 parts.

Fluency and Coherence	6
Lexical Resource	6
Grammatical Range and Accuracy	6
Pronunciation	7

Estimated IELTS Speaking Band   **6**

SPEAKING PRACTICE TEST 13

Examiner's Commentary

The person interviewed is Deniz, a Turkish female. Deniz is a graphic designer.

Part 1

Deniz spoke fluently and confidently. She used vocabulary and grammar flexibly and accurately and has the ability to use longer and complex sentences without difficulty. She speaks with an accent, but this is not intrusive. There were occasional errors ("more green" instead of "greener" or "but if it is a grocery" or "it might help you to growth" instead of "grow"), but these did not affect communication. Deniz also uses English in a colloquial way at appropriate times, which makes her sound very comfortable with using English. There were occasional pauses as she accessed vocabulary, but she interacted well with the examiner to ensure that she was understood.

Part 2

Deniz chose a good subject for her Part 2. It was a famous place and allowed her to talk at length. She spoke a long time, in spite of the fact that she speaks quite quickly. Again her vocabulary, grammar and general communicative ability were very good. There were again errors ("Once in a year" instead of "once a year"), but again these did not impede communication. Deniz's accent was still apparent, but she spoke clearly and the occasional word or phrase seemed by her pronunciation that she has spent some time in a native English-speaking country.

Part 3

Deniz gave long and complex answers for Part 3 and showed she had the language ability to discuss more complex ideas. It helped that she had studied architecture, but this does not necessarily mean that she would have the vocabulary range in English that she clearly has. Again, all aspects of Deniz's English were very good.

Marking - The marking of the IELTS Speaking Test is done in 4 parts.

Fluency and Coherence	7
Lexical Resource	7
Grammatical Range and Accuracy	7
Pronunciation	8
Estimated IELTS Speaking Band	**7**

SPEAKING PRACTICE TEST 14

Examiner's Commentary

The person interviewed is Shaifali, a Singaporean female. Shaifali is a student.

Part 1

Right from the start, Shaifali showed that she had an excellent command of English; she spoke fluently, confidently and idiomatically. Shaifali gave full and intelligent answers to all questions and did not hesitate to access language or structure. Shaifali's grammar was very accurate and there were no errors. Her word choice was also automatic and highly appropriate in all speeches. Shaifali did not seem to have any interference in her accent at all from a mother tongue. Shaifali also used humour in appropriate situations.

Part 2

Shaifali showed again in Part 2 her strong ability in English and she had no problem speaking at length. Although an extremely strong candidate, she still took the whole minute available to prepare her talk, which is always highly advisable. Shaifali spoke fluently and again with humour and showed that she could perform a long turn without any problems at all. Again her vocabulary and grammar ranges were excellent and she did not make any errors at all.

Part 3

The greater demands of Part 3 only allowed Shaifali to show her excellent standard of English. She spoke sensitively and coherently with the more difficult questions, without any errors coming into her English. Her pronunciation remained impeccable and of a native speaker standard.

Marking - The marking of the IELTS Speaking Test is done in 4 parts.

Fluency and Coherence	9
Lexical Resource	9
Grammatical Range and Accuracy	9
Pronunciation	9
Estimated IELTS Speaking Band	**9**

SPEAKING PRACTICE TEST 15

Examiner's Commentary

The person interviewed is Teresita, a Philippine female. Teresita is a nurse.

Part 1

Teresita spoke very fluently and confidently. Her speech was very clear and her accent was hardly apparent. Her sentences were well constructed and her lexis were varied and reasonably idiomatic. There were some grammar errors with article problems being apparent. Occasionally there were some grammar and lexis problems with sentences carrying some wrong or awkward choices (e.g.: "that their team had that loss). Teresita's answers were fairly full and she was good at adding detail to her comments.

Part 2

Teresita underperformed in this Part. She spoke only for 30 seconds and the examiner had to prompt her to address some of the questions on the card. Teresita did not use her minute's preparation and seemed over-confident. By not reading what was required of her, she did not speak for long enough and did not show her English abilities. What English she did produce showed again that she was a strong English user, though she did make some errors.

Part 3

A good performance here, though Teresita still showed that she has problems with articles. She showed her good vocabulary and grammar range. Teresita still needed to develop answers a bit more fully, as it sometimes gave the impression that she did not have the language to do so. This resulted in Part 3 being a little shorter than it should have been. At the end, Teresita did not clearly listen to the question. When asked how education prepares young people for technology today, Teresita talked about how young people need to learn when to use their phones.

Marking - The marking of the IELTS Speaking Test is done in 4 parts.

Fluency and Coherence	7
Lexical Resource	7
Grammatical Range and Accuracy	7
Pronunciation	8
Estimated IELTS Speaking Band	**7**

Listening Recordings' Transcripts

LISTENING TEST 11 TRANSCRIPT

This recording is copyright by Robert Nicholson and Simone Braverman, all rights reserved.

IELTS listening practice tests. Test eleven. In the IELTS test you hear some recordings and you have to answer questions on them. You have time to read the instructions and questions and check your work. All recordings are played only once. The test is in four parts. Now turn to part one.

Part one. You will hear a conversation between a man and a woman as the woman buys a new bus pass.

First you have some time to look at questions one to five.

(20 second gap)

Now we begin. You should answer the questions as you listen, as the recording is not played twice. Listen carefully to the conversation and answer questions one to five.

David	Good morning, Madam. How can I help you?
Louise	Hi there. My name's Louise. I need to get a new bus pass.
David	Do you know which zones you'll need it for?
Louise	Yes. Zones one, two and three.
David	That's fine. Now, have you had a bus pass before?
Louise	Yes, I've had one for the last <u>six months</u> **(Q1)** and it expired today.
David though.	That's good. I won't need to take your details then. I'll need to confirm some information
Louise	That's fine.
David	Can you let me know your postcode?
Louise	It's NW thirteen, four SG.
David	And can you let me know the number of the house at that postcode?
Louise	It's number thirteen.
David still right?	I've got your records here. It says that we should contact you on your mobile phone. Is that
Louise current address.	I'd like to change that actually to <u>email</u> **(Q2)**. I've not changed it, so you should have my

David	Let's see. Is it louise k at UK net dot com?

Louise	That's right.

David	OK. I've made a note of that.

Louise	I won't get extra spam, will I?

David	No, don't worry. Our data policy specifies that we can't pass on your information to anyone or contact you without good reason.

Louise	Good. Thank you.

David	Now on your old bus pass, there was no <u>photo **(Q3)**</u>. The new one will be a photocard. Do you have a photo with you?

Louise	No, I don't. I didn't know that I would need it.

David	That's OK. We put the requirement on the website, but of course most people don't see it. I can take it here if you like. Just look at this screen.

Louise	Like this?

David	That's right. Now keep still. OK. That's done.

Louise	By the way, is the price still a hundred pounds?

David	I'm afraid not. The price went up by <u>five per cent **(Q4)**</u>. It's still pretty good value though.

Louise	Yes. That's fine.

David	So, here's your new pass and here's a new holder. I saw that your old one had got bit worn.

Louise	Yes, it had. Thanks very much. The old one had gotten a bit beaten up, being at the bottom of my bag all the time.

David	One more thing. I noticed there was no <u>signature **(Q5)**</u> on the back of your old bus pass. It isn't valid without it, so you'd better do that now to your new one.

Louise	Oh, I didn't know that either. I'll do it now. There you are.

Before the conversation continues, you have some time to look at questions six to ten.

(20 second gap)

Now listen carefully and answer questions six to ten.

David	Is there anything else I can help you with?

Louise	Yes, there is actually. You know that all the bus routes have been reorganised recently.

David   Yes.

Louise   Well, I'm a bit confused. Could you briefly explain some of the changes?

David   Of course. First of all, there is route one. That's the one that goes in the direction of the town hospital when it goes north and the university when it goes south. There are two bus stops where you can get on this. To go north, you need to find bus stop Q. That's on Alton Road, just outside the town hall. **(Q6)** To go south, towards the university, then find bus stop P, which is also on Alton Road, outside the cinema.

Louise   That's useful for me, as I study at the university. Now I live in West Howe. What will I need to do to get a route one bus?

David   The best way is to go to the town centre and change. You'll need to take route three. Take the bus from the centre of West Howe and get off at the town centre at bus stop G. That's outside West Gate Shopping Centre. **(Q7)** Then, to get back to West Howe, you'll need to go back to West Gate Shopping Centre and find bus stop H, opposite bus stop G.

Louise   Thanks. Finally, I need to know how to get to the Arrowdown Sports Centre. I was given a membership there and so I'll be going there quite often too.

David   First of all, you need to come to the centre of town, as you would normally. Then to get to that sports centre, you'll need to go to the town centre post office. The buses for the Arrowdown Centre are from bus stop A. **(Q8)** To get back, take the bus from outside the sports centre and get off at bus stop C in the town centre.

Louise   Thanks for that. Now, a friend told me that I can get discounts using my bus pass. He said that I can get cheaper cinema tickets and train tickets with it.

David   I'm afraid not with the cinema, but you'll get a fifteen per cent discount on local train services. **(Q9)** There are other possibilities as well. The local football club gives you access to the special hospitality area, although you'll need to buy a regular ticket. You can also get priority seating at the local theatre and the local museum gives bus pass holders cheaper entry. **(Q10)** Some of these things are restricted by availability, of course.

Louise   Well, that's a bonus!

That is the end of part one. You will now have half a minute to check your answers.

(30 second gap)

Now turn to part two.

Part two. You will hear a man giving an information talk at an adult education centre. First you have some time to look at questions eleven to fifteen.

(20 second gap)

Now listen carefully to the information talk and answer questions eleven to fifteen.

Good evening everyone and thanks for coming to this information evening at the Adult Education Centre. My name is Mike and I'll be speaking to you for a short while before you can go and explore the various departments that we have here.

The centre was founded fifty years ago by <u>the town council **(Q11)**</u> in order to help people who had failed to get a proper education when they were children. The idea today is a little different. We can give people the chance to study what they missed at school for whatever reason, but we can also just give them training in everyday skills or just allow them to extend themselves.

The teachers in the centre are fully qualified and their teaching is appraised <u>every six months **(Q12)**</u> by inspectors from the Ministry of Education. Our teachers have the latest teaching aids and accessories, from interactive whiteboards to computer labs with the most up-to-date technology. All our teachers undergo special training and all their lessons can be found online at what we call <u>the interactive classroom, **(Q13)**</u> which is accessible by all registered students. All notes, videos and worksheets can be found there, so if you miss a lesson, you can catch up on your computer at home. As well as just finding the resources, you can be in direct contact with your teacher. Naturally, he or she cannot be online all day, but every teacher has two online tutorial sessions of <u>three hours **(Q14)**</u> each when they are available to chat. They can of course be in demand, so they are limited to four students at any one time and students can only interact with their teacher for a maximum of ten minutes. If the teacher is free though, students may continue to chat for longer.

Naturally, we also have a normal website. This has details of all our courses, teachers, fees and timetables. All courses can be booked and paid for online, although you'll need of course to supply credit card or bank account details. If you don't want to book online, you'll need to come to our main centre on Langdon Street between the hours of ten a.m. and <u>two p.m. **(Q15)**</u>, which are the hours that our administration section is open to the general public.

You now have some time to look at questions sixteen to twenty.

(20 second gap)

Now listen to the rest of the information talk and answer questions sixteen to twenty.

Now let me tell you a little about the courses that we have on offer. I'll begin with languages, as they're often very popular. We offer a variety of European languages, including French, German, Polish and Spanish. In addition, we offer Arabic, Korean, Japanese and Mandarin Chinese. These languages are offered at various stages of ability and to find out which class you belong in, you can do our <u>self-assessment test **(Q16)**</u> available on our website for all the languages we offer.

Next, I'd like to tell you about our business related courses. Our business courses vary from short morning or afternoon sessions, where you will develop an excellent understanding of a particular topic, to courses that run for over thirty weeks, where you can achieve an industry-recognised qualification. From learning how to use essential computer software to bookkeeping **(Q17)** or search engine optimisation and website development, we have the business courses to help you achieve your goals. These courses are always the most popular, so if you're interested, make sure you make your booking fast. We only take ten people per course and these places go quickly.

One of our most popular course areas is photography and computers for photography **(Q18)**. Our range of courses on these subjects can help you learn to get the most out of your camera. From basic to advanced, our courses will allow you to build up your knowledge and learn new ways to use your equipment.

Another favourite are our cooking courses. We offer speciality courses, but a favourite is our introduction to cooking. This course is ideal for those new to cooking or for anyone wishing to create achievable and inspiring dishes. Learn a variety of essential cooking techniques to help you create simple everyday dishes or some more elaborate things to impress your guests. You will also learn to make the best use of store cupboard ingredients, and how to take delicious shortcuts **(Q19)** to make cooking quick and enjoyable every day.

I'll finish with telling you about our creative writing course. It looks at practical ways to get started, whilst promoting greater writing confidence. The focus of this course is placed on practical exercises supported by discussion and examples and builds upon the strengths of each writer. It will give you an insight into the creative process and encourage you to achieve your writing goals. Our creative writing course provides an opportunity for all aspiring writers to develop the skills **(Q20)** for writing fiction.

We have lots more courses and I urge you to check our website, as we don't have enough time to introduce everything that we have on offer.

That is the end of part two. You will now have half a minute to check your answers.

(30 second gap)

Now turn to part three.

Part three. You will hear four students discussing a survey that they will conduct. First you have some time to look at questions twenty-one to twenty-six.

(20 second gap)

Now listen carefully and answer questions twenty-one to twenty-six.

Abbie	Hi Martin. Hi Rachel. Are you both waiting for us?
Martin	Hi Abbie. Hi Lance. Yes, we are, but we've not been waiting long.
Rachel	Yes. We just ordered some coffee. Hi Lance.
Lance	Hi everyone.

Martin   So, we're here today to talk about our survey on electronics and communications. Rachel, you said you were going to think about some question ideas.

Rachel   That's right. I've been looking at our subject of how household citizens in this country derive benefit from the digital environment. To start with, I thought we could ask about their perceptions of Internet speed.

Lance   Dial-up or broadband?

Rachel   Broadband **(Q21)** I think, Lance. Not many people in this country have dial-up any more.

Abbie   I think that's a great start, Rachel. It's very topical at the moment. What about after that?

Rachel   Another important area is people's perceptions of affordability. This has a lot to do whether people have travelled to different countries and have seen the costs of services there and are therefore able to compare what they pay for here.

Lance   That's not necessarily true, Rachel. People can have perceptions of affordability without having to have travelled.

Abbie   That's true, Lance. I like the idea, Rachel, but let's keep the travel part out of it. If we include that, we could create too much bias **(Q22)** within the answers, as people who don't travel wouldn't be able to answer.

Rachel   You're both right. I'll just make a note of that. Now, the next area I looked at was what people think about the possibility of changing subscriptions and switching between providers.

Martin   I thought it wasn't possible to just switch providers. Aren't people locked in with a contract?

Abbie   Yes, they are usually, but even within the contracts, there are ways of cancelling and changing provider.

Lance   There's also a lot of talk in the media about how many contracts demand three month notice periods **(Q23)**. People often don't realise that and they're furious when they have to wait and pay for three further months.

Abbie   Yes, I know someone in that position. They're actually leaving the country and they have to continue paying their communications bill for two months, when they're not even in the country or living at the address that the contract deals with.

Martin	Well, we should get some good feedback and answers on that area.

Rachel   So, my next area is the transparency of <u>tariff information</u> **(Q24)**. Again, this is a topical area in the communications industry.

Lance   That's right. There were some big stories in the media recently. The government has clamped down on companies not disclosing this.

Martin   I read a story last week about a family that sued their phone provider for not giving the proper information. The family won and it seems the government has finally woken up about this matter and will do something about it.

Abbie   Why is it so important?

Martin   It's because companies want people to choose the package that gives them the most <u>profit</u> **(Q25)**. It doesn't matter to them that people don't get the deal that makes the most sense for them. Salespeople just give customers a limited number of options and customers can't find the full information anywhere else.

Abbie   That's awful. I can't believe they can get away with that nowadays.

Martin   I know. Fortunately, things are getting better though.

Rachel   So, the last area is about mobile phone usage.

Abbie   Will we just be looking at how often people use their mobile phones?

Rachel   Not so much that. We'll be more interested in how happy customers are with their <u>signal reception</u> **(Q26)**.

Lance   That's a good topic too. I thought that we had good coverage in this country, but then I heard from some foreign student friends of mine that it's terrible here and that their countries are much better.

Rachel   That's right. We think it's OK here, as we're used to nothing different.

You now have some time to look at questions twenty-seven to thirty.

(20 second gap)

Now listen to the rest of the discussion and answer questions twenty-seven to thirty.

Lance   So, next we have to decide when and where to do our survey.

Abbie   I think the best thing would be to go after lectures on Wednesday morning. We'd get the afternoon shoppers and we'd get it all done before dinner.

Rachel   The problem with that is we'd only get people free on a weekday afternoon. There would be a lot of unemployed people and that would influence the results. On a Saturday afternoon, we'd get a lot more people and a better cross-section of society.

Abbie   I don't really want to lose my Saturday though.

Martin   Nor do I. I want to go to the football. Can't we do Friday afternoon? There'll be lots of people around off work early then.

Lance   Well, that would be better than Wednesday, but I think Rachel's right. Nobody wants to work at weekends, but if we want to do a good job with this survey, then we should make some sacrifices.

Abbie   OK.

Martin   Yes, I suppose the football can wait **(Q27)**.

Lance   Now, are we sure that the town centre is the best place to conduct our survey? What do you think, Rachel?

Rachel   Well, it's the place where we'd find the most people. Also, we'd probably find the best cross-section of society there.

Martin   The trouble as I see it is that some people won't want to be stopped to answer our questions. You know what it's like.

Abbie   That's true, but that will be the same wherever we go. The other places where we'd find lots of people could be worse. In train and bus stations, people would be busy. I think Rachel's idea about the town centre is best.

Lance   What about in the central shopping mall?

Rachel   Again, maybe there would be too many of a certain type of people.

Martin   OK. I'm fine with Rachel's idea.

Lance   Me too. I'm happy **(Q28)**.

Abbie   Finally, we need to analyse the information as fast as possible. Why don't you all come round to my place the next day and we can collate everything and do some statistical analysis **(Q29)**. Can you make that, Lance?

Lance   I can't after three o'clock. I have to be with my family then. I could come before that or in the evening.

Abbie   How about you, Rachel?

Rachel   That should be no problem for me, as I'm free all day, so just let me know when. What about you, Martin?

Page 158

Martin   It might be a problem for me, I'm afraid. I can come, but not in the evening. I've got tickets to the <u>cinema</u> **(Q30)**.

Abbie   Let's meet at midday then. We should be able to get everything done in a couple of hours, so Lance can get away.

That is the end of part three. You will now have half a minute to check your answers.

(30 second gap)

Now turn to part four.

Part four. You will hear a lecture on geothermal energy. First you have some time to look at questions thirty-one to forty.

(50 second gap)

Now listen carefully and answer questions thirty-one to forty.

Hello everyone and welcome to this lecture on renewable energy resources. Today, we're going to look at geothermal energy and we'll look at the country of Iceland to see how this energy type has been exploited there.

Geothermal energy is the heat from the Earth. It's clean and sustainable. Resources of geothermal energy range from the shallow ground to hot water and hot rock found a few miles beneath the Earth's surface, and down even deeper to the layer of extremely high temperature magma. This layer of magma continually produces heat, mostly from the <u>decay</u> **(Q31)** of naturally radioactive materials, such as uranium and potassium. The amount of heat within ten thousand meters of Earth's surface contains fifty thousand times more energy than all the oil and natural gas resources in the world.

Iceland is a pioneer in the use of geothermal energy for space heating. Generating electricity with geothermal energy has also increased significantly in recent years. Geothermal power facilities currently generate twenty-five per cent of the country's total electricity output. Last year, roughly eighty-four per cent of primary energy use in Iceland came from indigenous renewable resources, of which sixty-six per cent was geothermal. During the course of the twentieth century, Iceland went from what was one of Europe's lowest income countries, dependent upon peat and imported coal for its energy, to a country with a premier <u>standard of living</u> **(Q32)**, where most energy is derived from renewable resources. The cheap source of energy created this change.

Iceland is a young country geologically. It lies astride one of the Earth's major fault lines, the Mid-Atlantic ridge. This is the boundary between the North American and Eurasian tectonic plates. The two plates are moving apart at a rate of about <u>two</u> **(Q33)** centimetres per year. Iceland is an anomalous part of the ridge, where deep mantle material wells up and creates a hot spot of unusually great volcanic productivity. This makes Iceland one of the few places on Earth where one can see an active spreading ridge above sea level.

Page 159

As a result of its location, Iceland is one of the most geologically active places on Earth, resulting in a large number of volcanoes and hot springs. Earthquakes **(Q34)** are also frequent, but rarely cause serious damage. More than two hundred volcanoes are located within the active volcanic zone, stretching through the country from the southwest to the northeast, and at least thirty of them have erupted since the country was settled.

A lot of Iceland's geothermal energy comes from hot water or steam and these are found in two types of water temperature systems, high temperature fields and low temperature fields. High temperature fields are located within the active volcanic zones **(Q35)** or marginal to them. They are mostly on high ground and the rocks are geologically very young and permeable. As a result of the topography and high bedrock permeability, the groundwater table in the high temperature areas is generally deep, and surface manifestations are largely steam vents **(Q36)**.

The low temperature fields are all located outside the volcanic zone passing through Iceland. The largest examples of these systems are located in southwest Iceland, on the flanks of the western volcanic zone, but smaller systems can be found throughout the country. On the surface, low temperature activity is manifested in hot or boiling springs, although no surface indications are observed on top of some such systems. Flow rates range from almost zero to a maximum of one hundred and eighty litres per second from a single spring. Scientists believe these low temperature fields are transient **(Q37)**, lasting some thousands of years.

There are three ways to create electricity with geothermal energy. Hydrothermal, using hot water, geopressurised, using a hydraulic turbine, and petrothermal, using superheated dry rock to create steam when water is pumped into it. In Iceland, generating electricity with geothermal energy has increased significantly in recent years and as a result of a rapid expansion in Iceland's energy intensive industry, the demand for electricity has increased considerably. One of the most common electricity generation methods in Iceland is with a geothermal plant, which brings heat up to the surface, where it is brought into contact with water. This creates high pressure steam, which is then piped to drive turbines. The pipes and turbines must be extremely strong in order to stop the corrosive steam **(Q38)** from bursting out and causing a danger to workers. The turbines in turn create the electromagnetic field within a generator that creates electricity. The electricity generated is then transferred out to a local substation **(Q39)**, before being directed to its place of end use. Back at the geothermal plant, the steam that has been through the turbines is piped away. The steam is then allowed to condense in a cooling tower **(Q40)**. Warm air and vapour is released into the air and the left-over hot water is piped away for a variety of other direct heat uses, such as house heating, agriculture, fish farms and industry.

That is the end of part four. You will now have half a minute to check your answers.

(30 second gap)

That is the end of listening test eleven.

LISTENING TEST 12 TRANSCRIPT

This recording is copyright by Robert Nicholson and Simone Braverman, all rights reserved.

IELTS listening practice tests. Test twelve. In the IELTS test you hear some recordings and you have to answer questions on them. You have time to read the instructions and questions and check your work. All recordings are played only once. The test is in four parts. Now turn to part one.

Part one. You will hear a conversation between a man and a woman as they discuss a hiking holiday in Scotland.

First you have some time to look at questions one to five.

(20 second gap)

Now we begin. You should answer the questions as you listen, as the recording is not played twice. Listen carefully to the conversation and answer questions one to five.

Graham	So, Sophie. Are you ready to talk about our holiday in Scotland?
Sophie	Oh yes. I'm looking forward to getting things finalised.
Graham	So, we start our holiday in Oban, then we go to Skye and after that to Lewis.
Sophie	That's right.
Graham	Now, <u>we're staying in Oban for five nights from the eighth of July</u> **(Q1)** until the thirteenth. Is that right?
Sophie	I thought we were one day earlier. Let's have a look. No, you're right. It's from the eighth. It's my grandmother's birthday on the seventh and I got mixed up.
Graham	Good, that's settled then. It wouldn't have been a good start if we got the dates wrong!
Sophie	No. I remember that I wanted to be at home for grandma's birthday and that we could leave the next day.
Graham	So, the next thing should be how we're going to get to Oban.
Sophie	Well, as I see it, we have the choice of driving up, the train or the bus.
Graham	Yes. Driving up wouldn't be the cheapest, but it would be the fastest. However, as we're going on a hiking holiday, we won't need the car at all after we've arrived.
Sophie	And as we're taking the ferry to Lewis, it'll be cheaper not to have the car and travel as foot passengers.
Graham	The bus would be convenient then, as it takes us straight to Oban with only one change.
Sophie	The train does as well.
Graham	<u>That's true, though I checked and if we book the bus in advance, the train will be twice as expensive.</u>

Page 161

Sophie	Well, let's go for the cheapest option then. The bus won't be that much longer. Are you OK with that? **(Q2)**
Graham	Yes, that's fine. We can use the money we save on spoiling ourselves when we're there!
Sophie	So, what's next?
Graham	We have to decide on where we're going to stay.
Sophie	Yes. Now, you know I said I'd check some places out?
Graham	Yes. You said that you would order some magazines.
Sophie	Well, I had a look at some places online, but I didn't have much time and I didn't manage to do anything else **(Q3)**.
Graham	That's OK. Don't worry. I know that you were really busy.
Sophie	Yes. I had good intentions, but they didn't work out.
Graham	So, now we have to decide what kind of place we want to stay in. The choice is really a hostel, a guest house or a hotel.
Sophie	I'm tired of staying in cheap hostels and I've had a look at the guest houses and there's not a great selection.
Graham	I agree. So, we'll go for a hotel then. **(Q4)**
Sophie	Yes. We can use the money we saved on the travel!
Graham	OK. Now, do you want to have breakfast and dinner at the hotel?
Sophie	I'd say so. It would be very convenient. Breakfast would be waiting for us every morning and in the evenings we'd be tired after our hiking and not too keen to go out.
Graham	That's true, but Oban has great places to eat and I think we should make the effort to get out in the evenings and try some places. Oban's small and nothing will be too far away.
Sophie	OK. I'll go along with that. I still think breakfast would be better at the hotel though.
Graham	Yes, I agree with that. **(Q5)**

Before the conversation continues, you have some time to look at questions six to ten.

(20 second gap)

Now listen carefully and answer questions six to ten.

Sophie   So, have you researched any hiking routes when we get to Oban?

Graham   Yes, I've looked at a few. My favourite one is a coastal route that goes from Oban to a small town called Dunbeg.

Sophie   Tell me about it.

Graham   It's a nice easy one to start with. This is because we stick to the coast, so there are no <u>hills</u> **(Q6)** to deal with. We'd start after breakfast and head north and move up and hug the coast. The hike will take about three and a half hours and the end point is Dunbeg, which is inland a little.

Sophie   Are there any good things to see?

Graham   Yes. There are the views of the sea and of course the island of Kerrera, across from Oban. Soon we'll pass Saint Columba's cathedral and near the end of the walk, there's a spectacular ruined castle next to the sea. At the end, we can get a <u>bus</u> **(Q7)** back from Dunbeg.

Sophie   How long does the bus take?

Graham   Only about a quarter of an hour. We can walk back the way we came or walk back along the road, but I thought it would be nice to have lunch in Dunbeg and then get back to Oban quickly and spend the afternoon looking around the town.

Sophie   That all sounds fine. Have you found any other hikes?

Graham   You know I mentioned the island of Kerrera earlier?

Sophie   Yes.

Graham   Well, for the second day's hike we can get a ferry across to the island from Oban and there are a number of routes there. The easiest and most popular route is the southern one and again we'll get to see a castle.

Sophie   Is it a demanding route?

Graham   Not at all. The hike is approximately <u>five</u> **(Q8)** miles in total and I think it will take us at least three hours for it. The island is mostly flat and the path is well-tended. It shouldn't stretch us very much.

Sophie   I expect there'll be a lot of sea views again being an island. I really like that.

Graham   Actually not as much as you'd think, as we'll be going inland a lot.

Sophie   We'll have seen a lot of the sea the day before, so that's fine.

Graham   That's what I thought.

Sophie   Good. I'll be quite unfit and I want to break into things slowly. We can go for harder hikes later in the holiday.

Graham   Exactly. So, to make this hike into a day trip, we can look around the castle, as it was restored a few years ago. We can also take a <u>picnic **(Q9)**</u> and relax next to a good view.

Sophie   Well, that's the first two days then. Now, the first hike should be easy to find our way, as we're just following the coastline, but the second could be harder if we're going inland.

Graham   Yes, I thought about that. I went onto the island's website and we can buy a <u>map **(Q10)**</u> on the ferry while we're crossing over.

Sophie   Oh good. Well done. You seem to have done some good research.

Graham   Thanks. I'm quite excited about our trip.

That is the end of part one. You will now have half a minute to check your answers.

(30 second gap)

Now turn to part two.

Part two. You will hear a woman telling a group information about a museum tour. First you have some time to look at questions eleven to fifteen.

(20 second gap)

Now listen carefully to the information talk and answer questions eleven to fifteen.

Good afternoon everyone and welcome to this tour of the Weyport museum. My name is Victoria and I'll be showing you round today. This will be a two-hour tour and I'll show you all the key exhibits that we possess. Naturally, we won't be able to look at everything, but the museum will remain open for three hours after the tour ends, so you'll be able to see anything you missed then.

The building that the museum stands in today has been here since the late nineteenth century. It was built by the local Weyport town council and owned by them until ten years ago, although the use of the building changed several times during their ownership. Ten years ago, the town council allowed the building to be bought by a group of enthusiasts that had been canvassing for a larger and better-equipped town museum for quite a few years. <u>They had gained cash from a variety of fund raising activities that were supported by the general public **(Q11)**.</u> The existing small museum was happy to merge with the new one and allow the new one to take all the exhibits and the previous museum director continued in his post at the new museum. <u>The new museum's purchase was also assisted financially by the local engineering company **(Q12)**,</u> Ryland Limited, whose managing director is a great patron of the arts. At first, the local council wasn't too keen on letting go of the building, but the central arts council in London liked the idea of the new museum and applied some administrative pressure. The local council agreed and the sale went through fairly quickly.

As I said, the history of the building was varied. <u>It started off as an office administration centre for the local council **(Q13)**.</u> Unfortunately, there was a fire in nineteen twenty and after that, the building lay unused for a number of years. There was a lack of funds for renovation, in spite of the insurance pay out. <u>From nineteen thirty, the building was made safe and used as a storage facility for old files and other</u>

Page 164

<u>records belonging to the town council **(Q14)**.</u> The army tried to gain control of the building to use as a recruitment centre during World War Two, but the building was deemed too unsafe for the projected numbers of people. After the war, the building continued its pre-war use until the nineteen sixties, when <u>the council used the building for its local education department **(Q15)**.</u> The building remained like this until it was sold for the new museum. The education department moved to the new council offices on the edge of town and is found next to the housing department.

You now have some time to look at questions sixteen to twenty.

(20 second gap)

Now listen to the rest of the information talk and answer questions sixteen to twenty.

So, we'll begin the tour on the ground floor. Right now, we're in the reception hall where you all bought your tickets. We've just come in through the main doors with the ticket office opposite. <u>We'll start by going in through the door on the right. If you go left, you'll find the museum's bathrooms. **(Q16)**</u> You'll need to come back here if you want to use them.

<u>So, in this first room on the right, we'll find our collections of paintings **(Q17)**.</u> We have mostly pictures by local painters. No one is particularly famous, but the quality is very high and we get visitors from all over the country. <u>We continue the tour into the next two rooms, where we will find very unusual exhibitions. This town is famous for its factories that manufacture clocks and silverware. The clock collection from the local factories comes first and then the following room focuses on silverware **(Q18)**. In the corner of the silverware room, there is a room where you can see a film **(Q19)**</u> that explains the history of both our town's famous industries.

Moving round into the next room, we'll find displays from the town's Iron Age history. There are examples of a variety of things that have been discovered in and around the town. We have old pots, jewelry, weapons, examples of surviving architecture and plenty of photographs of local archaeological sites. The next room houses the museum's café, where you can get hot or cold drinks and some snacks to eat. <u>Finally, the last room on the ground floor holds our collection of antique children's toys **(Q20)**.</u> It's amazing to see the range of things that were manufactured and this room is always a favourite with visitors. After we've finished there, we'll move up the stairs to the first floor, where we'll continue.

That is the end of part two. You will now have half a minute to check your answers.

(30 second gap)

Now turn to part three.

Part three. You will hear three students discussing a field trip. First you have some time to look at questions twenty-one to twenty-five.

(20 second gap)

Now listen carefully and answer questions twenty-one to twenty-five.

Ellie	Hi Alan.
Alan	Hi Ellie. Hi Janet. How are you both today?

Janet	Hi Alan. We're both good. Are you ready to discuss our field trip?
Alan	Sure. That's why I'm here.
Ellie	Good. Let's get started. We're going to go on a trip down the coast to look at cliff formations. We know the date we're going, so <u>the first thing is that we need to decide how to get there **(Q21)**</u>.
Alan	Yes. The options are hiring a car for the day or getting the bus. The car will be more flexible, but the bus will be cheaper.
Janet	I'll go down to the bus station this afternoon and check prices and times and then I'll go to that local car hire company next to the supermarket and get a quote.
Ellie	Good. Now, <u>we have the general area where we want to go, but we need to narrow down our survey area exactly **(Q22)**</u>.
Alan	I've had a look at the map. The best area would be from Durham Rocks to Long Beach.
Janet	Why there?
Alan	First of all, there's a car park and bus stop next to the Durham Rocks and there are also paths at the top of the cliff and at its foot at low tide along the beach. We'll get good access for our survey.
Ellie	Well done, Alan. <u>How long do you think the survey will take?</u>
Alan	<u>I reckon about five hours to do a good job. We won't need to stay overnight like some of the other groups. That's good, as there are no hostels or anything where we're going **(Q23)**</u>.
Janet	What things do we need to take with us?
Ellie	The usual survey stuff. <u>Maps, compasses, a level kit and a rangefinder.</u>
Janet	<u>Can we get all that?</u>
Ellie	<u>The department has it all and we can book it out as long as no one's got there first. I'll do that this afternoon when I go in for our lecture **(Q24)**</u>.
Alan	Thanks, Ellie.
Janet	<u>Is there any food available where we're going? We'll be there for quite some time and if things take longer than expected, we'll get hungry.</u>
Alan	<u>I'll check that out online. My laptop's at home right now, but I'll need to get it before my lecture. I'll do it when I get home. If there's nowhere to eat, I'll make some sandwiches and bring some water or something **(Q25)**</u>. I'll let you know at the lecture.
Ellie	Well, that's the organisation part done for the time being. Let's just hope it doesn't rain! I don't fancy spending five hours under an umbrella.

You now have some time to look at questions twenty-six to thirty.

(20 second gap)

Now listen to the rest of the discussion and answer questions twenty-six to thirty.

Janet   So, why are we going to that area of the coast anyway? There are plenty of cliffs much closer to us.

Alan   It's all to do with the erosion of the cliffs in that area. There are some really classic examples there. Do you remember that lecture we had on coastal erosion?

Janet   I missed that lecture, as I was sick.

Ellie   I'll explain. The cliffs in that area mostly consist of sand **(Q26)** and clay with very little rock. This makes them very susceptible to erosion.

Janet   Do all coastlines suffer from erosion?

Alan   It depends. Both exposed and sheltered coasts can suffer from it. The coast has to receive the power of the sea in a certain direction and force. Currents, winds and tides also play a key role.

Ellie   Where we're going, the sea comes right up to the cliffs at high tide **(Q27)**. The waves can then batter the soft lower parts of the cliffs. At low tide, we can walk in front of the cliffs for our survey.

Janet   Does that make it dangerous to walk at the top of the cliffs?

Alan   It can be. Fortunately, the area where we're going has paths set well back and there are fences to keep people away from edges that might be dangerous. We won't need to go close to the edges of the cliffs, anyway.

Janet   So, what happens when the waves hit the lower parts of the cliffs?

Ellie   It's simple really. The cliff is worn away and an undercut **(Q28)** is made. The deeper this becomes, the more unstable the cliff above becomes. When the weight above becomes too much, then the cliff collapses.

Alan   This of course can cause problems if there is anything significant on top of the cliffs.

Janet   It sounds like it's dangerous to be under the cliffs as well.

Alan   Yes, it is. The coastguard **(Q29)** is responsible for keeping a close eye on the cliffs though and you can check on the dangerous areas on their website. There are lots of signs in dangerous areas, too.

Janet   Before we go, we'd better check on that and the tides as well, as they can come in quickly.

Alan   I intend to.

Ellie   Don't worry, Janet. We won't go into any danger areas.

Janet   Should we take flares in case we get into any problems?

Alan   No, I don't think that's necessary. We'll all just take our mobile phones **(Q30)** with us. If we do run into any trouble, we can then call the authorities. It really won't be a problem, Janet. If I thought we'd be in any danger, I'd take an inflatable boat with us or not go at all!

That is the end of part three. You will now have half a minute to check your answers.

(30 second gap)

Now turn to part four.

Part four. You will hear a lecture on the Wechsler-Belleview Intelligence Scale. First you have some time to look at questions thirty-one to forty.

(50 second gap)

Now listen carefully and answer questions thirty-one to forty.

Good morning everyone and welcome to this psychology lecture. Today, we are going to look at one of the most common tests that is used to assess intelligence. Many tests have been created for this purpose, but we are focusing this morning on the Wechsler-Belleview Intelligence Scale.

Doctor David Wechsler, a clinical psychologist at New York's Belleview hospital, believed that intelligence is a global construct, reflecting a variety of measurable skills and should be considered in the setting of the <u>overall personality</u> **(Q31)**. Dissatisfied with the intelligence tests in vogue when he started practising, Wechsler created intelligence scales that included many novel concepts and breakthroughs to the intelligence testing movement. He did away with the quotient scores of older intelligence tests, or the Q in IQ. Instead, he assigned an arbitrary value of a hundred to the <u>mean</u> **(Q32)** intelligence and added or subtracted fifteen points for each standard deviation above or below the subject's mean.

The theoretical basis for the Wechsler-Belleview Intelligence Scale and the other Wechlser scales came from this belief of Wechsler's that intelligence is a complex ability involving a variety of skills. Because intelligence is multifaceted, Wechsler believed a test measuring intelligence must reflect this multitude of skills. Wechsler divided the concept of intelligence into two principal areas: <u>verbal</u> **(Q33)** and performance, and further subdivided and tested each area with a different subtest.

Wechsler's full scale test is broken down into fourteen sub-tests, comprising the verbal scale, seven verbal sub-tests, the performance scale and seven performance sub-tests. Wechsler's tests provide three scores: a verbal IQ score, a performance IQ score, and a composite IQ score based on the combined scores. Verbal subtests aim to test general cultural information, abstract comprehension, arithmetic, verbal reasoning, vocabulary, concentration, and memory. Performance subtests include visual perception, visual-motor coordination, spatial perception, abstract problem solving, sequential reasoning, perception speed, and visual analysis. These conceptualisations continue to be reflected in the Wechsler scales of the twenty-first century and the Wechsler-Belleview Intelligence Scale continues to remain the most commonly administered <u>psychological</u> **(Q34)** test in existence.

The Wechsler Adult Intelligence Scale is appropriate throughout adulthood. For testing children aged seven to sixteen, the Wechsler Intelligence Scale for Children is used, while the Wechsler Preschool and Primary Scale of Intelligence is used for testing children aged two and a half to seven. Both tests can be completed without a <u>literacy</u> **(Q35)** requirement in their subjects.

Although the Wechsler-Belleview Intelligence Scale is regarded as extremely useful and accurate, it does have some limitations. As long as test administrators realise this, the test can be used very reliably for its designed purposes. The limitations are not serious. It is not considered for measuring extremes of

intelligence, which are indicated by IQ scores below forty and above one hundred and sixty. Wechsler himself was even more conservative, stressing that his scales were not appropriate for people with an IQ below seventy or above one hundred and thirty. Also, when administering the Wechsler Adult Intelligence Scale to people at extreme ends **(Q36)** of the age range, such as below twenty years of age or above seventy, caution should be used for the interpretation **(Q37)** of scores.

Besides being used as an intelligence assessment, one other use of the Wechsler-Belleview Intelligence Scale is that it can be used for neuropsychological evaluation, as large differences in answers testing verbal and non-verbal intelligence may be a sign of specific sorts of brain damage **(Q38)**. Intelligence scores reported by the Wechsler-Belleview Intelligence Scale can also be used as part of the diagnostic criteria for learning disabilities and attention deficit hyperactivity disorder. However, the consensus of professionals in the field is that the Wechsler-Belleview Intelligence Scale is best used as a tool to evaluate intelligence and not to diagnose ADHD or learning disabled children. Nevertheless, many clinicians use it to compare a child's cognitive development to his or her actual social or school **(Q39)** capabilities. Using discrepancies in the scale and other sources of data, the Wechsler-Belleview Intelligence Scale can contribute information concerning a child's psychological well-being.

So, to conclude the first part of this lecture, the Wechsler-Belleview Intelligence Scale is regularly used by researchers in many areas of psychology as a measure of intelligence and it is considered to be a valid and reliable measure of general intelligence. It is so well regarded that other intelligence tests are often compared to it when undergoing reliability **(Q40)** and validity studies.

That is the end of part four. You will now have half a minute to check your answers.

(30 second gap)

That is the end of listening test twelve.

LISTENING TEST 13 TRANSCRIPT

This recording is copyright by Robert Nicholson and Simone Braverman, all rights reserved.

IELTS listening practice tests. Test thirteen. In the IELTS test you hear some recordings and you have to answer questions on them. You have time to read the instructions and questions and check your work. All recordings are played only once. The test is in four parts. Now turn to part one.

Part one. You will hear a conversation between a man and a woman discussing the enrollment of the man's child at a nursery.

First you have some time to look at questions one to five.

(20 second gap)

Now we begin. You should answer the questions as you listen, as the recording is not played twice. Listen carefully to the conversation and answer questions one to five.

Laura	Good morning. My name's Laura. Welcome to Happies Nursery. How can I help you today?
Luke	Good morning. My wife and I were hoping that we might be able to enrol our daughter with you.
Laura	We do have space, so that should be fine. What's the age of your daughter?
Luke	She's two.
Laura	OK. Now, I need to take some details first.
Luke	Of course.
Laura	To begin with, I need your and your wife's names.
Luke	My name is Luke Beckett and my wife's name is Gloria Beckett.
Laura	Would you spell Beckett for me, please?
Luke	It's B - E - C - K - E - T - T.
Laura	And Gloria?
Luke	G - L - O - R - I - A **(Q1)**.
Laura	Thank you. And can I assume that you both live together at the same address?
Luke	Yes, we do.
Laura	Can I have the full address?
Luke	It's forty **(Q2)** Castle Crescent. Backley.
Laura	And the post code?
Luke	It's BA three seven TR.

Laura	Thank you. Now, can I take some telephone numbers for you and your wife?

Luke	Of course. Our home number is oh one five three eight, eight five three, two eight five.

Laura	Thank you. And do you have mobile numbers?

Luke　　　　　Yes. Mine is oh seven seven seven oh, seven two eight four seven three and my wife's is oh seven seven four three, eight one two, <u>four five one</u> **(Q3)**.

Laura	Could you say your wife's again, please?

Luke	Of course. It's oh seven seven four three, eight one two, four five one.

Laura	Thanks. I've got all that down. Could I also have work numbers for you both?

Luke　　　　　My office number is oh one five three eight, nine two six, four seven seven and my wife's work number is oh one five three eight, five nine six, eight two one.

Laura　　　　　Thanks. Now, I'll talk about our fee structure a little later, but how would you like to pay our fees?

Luke	We'll pay by <u>bank transfer</u> **(Q4)** when we get the invoice.

Laura	That's fine. Thank you. So, your daughter. What's her name?

Luke	It's Gertrude Beckett. She has no middle name.

Laura	Good. She's two years old. I know that. Does she have any allergies that you know of?

Luke	The only one we know of is that she's allergic <u>to cats</u> **(Q5)**.

Laura　　　　　OK. I've made a note of that. It won't be a problem. There are no animals in our nursery and none of our teachers has a pet.

Luke	Good. That's very reassuring.

Before the conversation continues, you have some time to look at questions six to ten.

(20 second gap)

Now listen carefully and answer questions six to ten.

Laura　　　　　Now, I suppose you know quite a lot about us already, as you've chosen us to look after your daughter.

Luke	That's right. We have friends who have their children here.

Laura	That's good. I'd still like to talk about our systems here a little bit though.

Luke	Oh yes. That's fine.

Laura　　　　　So, we start doing activities at <u>eight thirty</u> **(Q6)** a.m., but parents can drop off their children at any time after six thirty. From six thirty, we always have a team of carers here who will supervise your child whilst she plays with the others and they will clean and change her when necessary. You don't need to bring anything in that regard, as we will have all that is necessary here.

Luke	Do we need to bring anything else for Gertrude?
Laura	Just a sweater for going outside and a couple of changes of <u>clothing</u> **(Q7)** in case she gets dirty. Keep it in a good quality bag and have it clearly marked as Gertrude's.
Luke	OK. What, what happens if Gertrude's sick?
Laura	We will of course call you and your wife straight away if she's sick. You'll need to pick her up as soon as you can when that happens, as we don't want other children to catch illnesses. In the unlikely event of anything really serious, we're just a mile away from the County Hospital. Also, we always have a <u>nurse</u> **(Q8)** on duty who specialises in children, so your child will always have good supervision in terms of health.
Luke	Good. Thank you.
Laura	The end of day-time activities is at four o'clock, though you can pick Gertrude up earlier if you wish. Also, we offer supervision until six thirty for people who work late. We ask that you do not arrive later than that to pick up your child, as our staff will want to get home to their families. If you're unavoidably detained, please call our number, which is in our <u>information pack</u> **(Q9)** here.
Luke	That shouldn't be a problem for us, as we both finish work at around four o'clock.
Laura	Good. Finally, I'd like to tell you about a new service that we're running. It will cost extra outside our usual fee structure, but it's proving to be incredibly popular. We now offer supervision at the <u>weekends</u> **(Q10)**, so that parents can be free to shop, travel a little or do other necessary things that would be awkward with a young child.
Luke	I don't think we'd need that often, as we wouldn't like to leave Gertrude then as we see her so little during the week. It would be very useful for unexpected things and emergencies though.
Laura	Well, let's move on to the fee structure.

That is the end of part one. You will now have half a minute to check your answers.

(30 second gap)

Now turn to part two.

Part two. You will hear a man giving some people information about an old age care centre. First you have some time to look at questions eleven to fifteen.

(20 second gap)

Now listen carefully to the information talk and answer questions eleven to fifteen.

Good morning everyone and welcome to this open day at the Green Trees Old Age Centre. My name is Charlie and I would like to tell you a little about us today. I have met some of you already and I know that some of you are thinking of coming to stay here yourselves and some of you are here to see it we will suit a friend or relative of yours.

So, we offer skilled elderly care for up to <u>sixty</u> **(Q11)** residents. We have places for both men and women, with men being accommodated on the first floor and women on the second floor. We have three lifts that service all the floors for those who find stairs challenging. All our rooms are single and therefore we are not suited to looking after married couples **(Q12)** together. All our rooms are en suite and are cleaned daily. Some types of pet are allowed, but this has to be discussed with the manager. The manager will decide on a case-by-case basis.

The common areas are exceptionally luxurious. We have lounges, television rooms and a games room, which are open to all residents. Our dining room is as well-appointed as the rest of our facilities and our food is exceptional. Breakfast, lunch and dinner are served of course every day and specialised diets **(Q13)**, for example for diabetics, can be catered for after consultation. If residents get hungry between meals, there is coffee and tea available mid-morning with snacks, and afternoon tea is served every day with sandwiches and cakes. In good weather in the summer, afternoon tea is served outside on the lawn.

One important part of any old age centre is our facilities for nursing. Older people need a special type of care the older they get and this must be combined with opportunities to retain the chances for being independent **(Q14)** as much as is practical. Green Trees has full-time nurses on duty twenty-four hours a day. These nurses have specialised in old age care and are all greatly experienced in this field. We also have access to extra specialised carers when the need arises. In addition to this, we have a local GP who visits twice a week. This GP is also able to visit at other times when necessary, including at night time.

Green Trees is a fee-charging establishment. I don't want to tell you all about our fees here, but all the details are available on our leaflets by the door and also on the website **(Q15)**. The fees advertised are our current ones, but be aware that fees change every six months, depending on our own costs.

You now have some time to look at questions sixteen to twenty.

(20 second gap)

Now listen to the rest of the information talk and answer questions sixteen to twenty.

Green Trees also has a variety of activities for our residents, both inside and outside our premises. Our activities provide our residents opportunities to have fun, exercise their brains and bodies, and meet new friends.

Twice weekly, we have sessions in our games room. This includes playing cards, bingo, board games, quizzes and lots of other activities. At Green Trees, we know it's important to meet different people and so residents are always allowed to invite a guest **(Q16)** to these evenings. In this way, everyone gets to meet new people and develop new friendships. We also have regular puzzle sessions at different times of the day, with crosswords, sudoku and other stimulating and fun activities. One exciting and new venture that we're doing right now is getting residents to tell their life stories. Sometimes it's not so easy to recall everything, but the attempt often brings back things previously forgotten. We also encourage the recollections to be recorded or written down, which is great for younger relatives, who find out things that they never would do otherwise. All these activities lead to fitness in the brain **(Q17)** for seniors and this has become an important part of lifelong well-being.

It's equally important to get out of Green Trees from time to time. We run regular visits to the theatre, ballet, opera, cinema, local markets and to places of local interest. We only organise one-day **(Q18)** trips, in case our residents get too tired. Family members can of course take residents out for overnight trips or longer whenever they want. We ask, of course, to be kept informed of any time spent away, so we can organize our food and care schedules accordingly.

One very popular activity in Green Trees is gardening. We have extended gardens and when the weather is appropriate, residents can change their clothes and go outside and get dirty! Gardening can be a very fulfilling activity for the elderly. Tending plants can overcome feelings of isolation **(Q19)** by giving individuals the opportunity to play a more active part in the world around them. Being responsible for the care of plants can also help residents feel more in control. The problem for a lot of elderly people is that manual work in the garden can cause serious aches and pains, whilst also worsening existing problems. We will give you training and the special tools **(Q20)** that will help you stay safe and healthy. Our two gardeners will also be there to supervise and give advice and I'm afraid residents also have to follow their orders about what is planted and where!

That is the end of part two. You will now have half a minute to check your answers.

(30 second gap)

Now turn to part three.

Part three. You will hear four students discussing their engineering work placements. First you have some time to look at questions twenty-one to twenty-five.

(20 second gap)

Now listen carefully and answer questions twenty-one to twenty-five.

Ross	Hi Tanya.
Tanya	Hi Ross, hi Derek.
Derek	Hi Tanya. Have you seen Lily?
Tanya	Yes, she's just behind me. Here she is.
Lily	Hi everyone.
Derek	Hi Lily. You know Ross, don't you?
Lily	Yes, I do. Hi Ross.
Ross	Hi Lily. So, Lily, do you know what you're doing for your engineering work placement?
Lily	Well, you know I applied for something in aviation engineering?
Ross	Yes.
Lily	Unfortunately, my application for that was turned down, so I also applied for a practical job, working on bridge construction in Brisbane.
Tanya	Was that successful?
Lily	No. They called and said someone else had taken the job, so I applied for a job helping in an engineering office in town.
Derek	So, that's what you're doing?

Page 174

| Lily | They offered me and I was about to accept when the bridge people called and said the person who'd accepted had dropped out, so I've ended up with that. **(Q21)** |

Lily   They offered me and I was about to accept when the bridge people called and said the person who'd accepted had dropped out, so I've ended up with that. **(Q21)**

Ross   Well done. You'll learn a lot with that.

Tanya   Yes, and it'll look great on your CV.

Lily   I'm sure it will. It's not aviation, but it'll still be very interesting. What about you, Ross?

Ross   Oh, I didn't have too much trouble. Fortunately my father has an engineering firm, so he's taken me on. **(Q22)**

Tanya   That should be great fun.

Ross   It might be, but you don't know my Dad. He'll work me to death. It might've been better just to have done some road surveying for the local government. That would've been boring, but at least nine to five.

Derek   I thought that you'd applied for work on an oil rig off Borneo.

Ross   I wanted to do that, but they said I didn't have the breadth of knowledge for working there. And Derek, what about your plans?

Derek   I had a placement working out in the Antarctic, but I had to turn it down.

Tanya   Oh no. Why?

Derek   I was worried about the extreme cold, but they said that I'd be OK with that. My Dad's a doctor in a hospital and he said that the months I was there would present no problems. However, my old trouble with blood circulation was noticed by the company supervisor working there and she said it was too big a risk being so far from a hospital, in case this came back. **(Q23)**

Tanya   That's a shame.

Derek   Yes, it is, but I've got a good placement in Brisbane's department of roads. That fits in with what I want to do when I graduate, so things worked out well in the end.

Lily   So, that leaves you, Tanya.

Tanya   I had three offers in the end.

Ross   Good for you. What were they?

Tanya   My tutor recommended working in a ship building yard, as he's got some contacts there. He said I'd get a really constructive job there. The second was in gas drilling, as my cousin works in that and he said he'd sort me out with something with him where I'd learn a lot. The last was for the city engineering department. My boyfriend works there and he wants me to be close.

Derek   Which did you choose?

Tanya   Well, I've always been interested in geology and the search for underground wealth, so I chose the one searching for gas. **(Q24)** That's the field I'd like to work in after graduation, although I'll find myself far away from any civilisation for most of my time. This one is right out in the desert.

Lily   By the way, how do we notify our department about our choices? Do we just call them or tell our tutors?

Ross   <u>There's an online form that needs to be printed out and filled in</u>. I don't think you <u>can send it as an attachment.</u>

Tanya   <u>Ross is right. It needs to be signed by your tutor and they need an original for their copy, so it needs to be given in face to face.</u> **(Q25)**

Derek   You'd think that nowadays they'd accept a scan of a signed document that was sent by email. I mean it's valid legally.

Lily   You know our professors. Some of them don't even know how to open their email!

You now have some time to look at questions twenty-six to thirty.

(20 second gap)

Now listen to the rest of the discussion and answer questions twenty-six to thirty.

Derek   So, Tanya, working in the desert! That'll be a bit scary, won't it?

Tanya   I expect when I go at the start, it'll be a bit frightening, but I've been told that you get used to it very quickly.

Ross   So, you're drilling for gas?

Tanya   That's right.

Lily   That sounds interesting. We haven't studied many things like that though.

Tanya   I know, so I've been studying it myself for a couple of months. The gas drilling station is a fairly standard assembly. The <u>well head</u> **(Q26)** is where the hole to the gas reservoir starts and it's above ground, next to a monitoring facility. That's where I'll be most of the time. The drill has to pass first through the normal earth until it hits a shale rock layer at around forty metres. After that, it passes through some <u>cap rock</u> **(Q27)** and finally some storage rock. Then it hits the gas reservoir.

Ross   Is it a long process?

Tanya   Quite long. The shale rock is easy to pass through, but the other layers are very hard and thick.

Derek   So, once the drill hits the gas reservoir, it's just a matter of monitoring.

Tanya   No. There's a constant need for working out how much gas is left and where the best place is to get it from. This means other holes may need to be drilled and that's what I'll be doing. We have secondary holes at different depths to the side of the primary drill hole and <u>underground sensors</u> **(Q28)** at the bottom send up information to the monitoring facility. This data then needs to be analysed.

Ross   It'll be a fantastic thing to do, Tanya. And it'll be great experience. If you want to work in that field later, it'll really help you find a job.

Lily   It'll be quite a lot of pressure on you also. You'll be in the desert with a few colleagues, making drilling decisions that will cost a lot of money.

Tanya   Not quite. We'll be analysing the data, but we'll be connected <u>by satellite</u> **(Q29)** to the head offices and it'll be the people there who make the decisions of whether to drill or not.

Lily   Oh good. That'll take the stress away. I'd hate to think what would happen if I had to make all the decisions out there.

Tanya   I don't think they'd let me do all the decision by myself in any situation. Anyway, it's not as if I'll be on my own out there!

Derek   Don't you think you'll go crazy being stuck out there in the desert? Our placements are for six months and after six months in the desert, I'd be feeling very strange.

Tanya   It won't be that bad. The teams that work out there are on four-week rotations. Everyone then gets a week off and then they go to a different station. My situation will be different. <u>After my four-week rotations, I'll be taken back to the city for four weeks and then I'll just do nine to five on weekdays at the head offices until I return to my drilling station</u> **(Q30)**. It's a good mixture. Back in the head offices, I'll be able to see what they do with the data that we collect out in the desert.

Ross   Well, that all sounds very exciting.

That is the end of part three. You will now have half a minute to check your answers.

(30 second gap)

Now turn to part four.

Part four. You will hear a lecture on hypnosis, hypnotism and hypnotherapy. First you have some time to look at questions thirty-one to forty.

(50 second gap)

Now listen carefully and answer questions thirty-one to forty.

Hello everyone. Today in our psychology lecture, we're going to look at hypnosis, hypnotism and hypnotherapy.

First of all, let's look at some definitions. Hypnosis is an inferred psychophysiological state characterised by greater possibilities for <u>influence</u> **(Q31)**, and is thought to be an altered state of consciousness. Hypnotism is the study and use of suggestion with the presence of hypnosis, while hypnotherapy, or clinical hypnosis, as it's sometimes referred to, is a form of therapy in which the use of hypnotism constitutes the core of the treatment. Simply speaking, hypnosis is an altered state of consciousness. Hypnotherapy, therefore, is the use of an altered state of consciousness, or trance, for a therapeutic endpoint. This means that people are not treated with hypnosis, but are treated in hypnosis.

All hypnotic states are characterised by a tremendously pleasant state of calm, which individuals allow themselves to enter, so that desired and beneficial suggestions may be given directly to the part of the mind known as the <u>subconscious</u> **(Q32)**. Under hypnosis, the conscious and rational part of the brain is temporarily avoided, making the subconscious part, which influences mental and physical functions, receptive to therapy. During the trance state, there is heightened <u>concentration</u> **(Q33)** for the specific purpose of maximising potential, changing limiting beliefs and behaviours and gaining insight and wisdom.

Although hypnosis may be light, medium or deep, a medium trance is usually used, during which breathing and the heartbeat slow and the brain produces alpha waves. Normal levels of consciousness, such as sleeping, dreaming or being awake, can be detected in the wave patterns produced by the brain. The state of hypnosis differs from all three. In alpha states, the body gradually achieves a particular relaxation **(Q34)**. Hypnosis, meditation, day dreaming, being absorbed in a book or music or television, driving and arriving at your destination without recalling all the usual hallmarks are good examples of alpha states.

It is still not well known how hypnosis influences the brain. One popular theory is that it affects the mechanisms of attention, which occurs in one area of the brain called the ascending reticular formation, located in the brain stem. This area, which has many functions related to sleep, alertness and the sensorial perception, continuously bombards the rest of the brain with stimuli coming from the sense organs **(Q35)**. The inhibition of the ascending reticular formation leads to states of extreme calm.

So, how does hypnotherapy work? The subconscious mind is the source of many of our problems and self images and our beliefs, habits and behaviours are stored there as information. The subconscious is a tremendous reservoir of our unrecognised strengths and knowledge. Hypnosis is a natural and effective technique for accessing the subconscious mind and the key to unleashing our potential **(Q36)**, so that we can change our unwanted habits and behaviours and find solutions to our problems and concerns. Once the individual has achieved a hypnotic trance state, the hypnotherapist uses many different therapeutic methods ranging from simple suggestions to psychoanalysis. For example, the therapist may ask about past, present or future concerns to establish the reasons for a particular problem. Alternatively, the therapist may give suggestions to the subconscious mind aimed at overcoming specific problems such as lack of self-confidence. While some uses, such as calming a person, need minimal change on the part of the individual, more complex behaviours, such as overeating, panic disorders or depression, require a more complex therapeutic intervention together with psychological homework **(Q37)**.

Hypnotherapy is a form of healing subject to much scepticism in the medical and scientific professions, in spite of it being conducted by qualified practitioners. Whilst it has often been clearly ascertained through various studies that a course of hypnotherapy can coincide with the improvement of a patient's medical condition, it is not simple to draw a direct correlation between that improvement and the process of hypnotherapy itself **(Q38)**. This is partly because there are few visible or extreme changes to metabolism during hypnotherapy. Further to this, patients react very differently and so a representative sample may not be all that representative at all. This makes it difficult to ascertain who reacts well to hypnotherapy and who just has a natural propensity to recover from the ailment that they were treated for. Many tests have shown that hypnotherapy has helped patients' conditions in conjunction with traditional medicine and that the effect of the hypnosis has only had a purely placebo basis. Patients therefore often have a positive mental response to treatment, but that this is only the patients' perception and is not due to the success of the treatment **(Q39)**. Finally, hypnotherapy is often criticised, because those criticising it have little knowledge of the processes and underlying methodology **(Q40)**.

Whilst there are doubts about the reliability of hypnotherapy as a method of healing, or, indeed as a method for helping people to deal with stress or to quit smoking, there seems no reason to doubt the effective results that it seems to produce in some patients.

That is the end of part four. You will now have half a minute to check your answers.
(30 second gap)

That is the end of listening test thirteen.

LISTENING TEST 14 TRANSCRIPT

This recording is copyright by Robert Nicholson and Simone Braverman, all rights reserved.

IELTS listening practice tests. Test fourteen. In the IELTS test you hear some recordings and you have to answer questions on them. You have time to read the instructions and questions and check your work. All recordings are played only once. The test is in four parts. Now turn to part one.

Part one. You will hear a conversation between a man and a woman as the woman books her son a place at a summer sports camp.

First you have some time to look at questions one to six.

(20 second gap)

Now we begin. You should answer the questions as you listen, as the recording is not played twice. Listen carefully to the conversation and answer questions one to six.

Mrs. Davis   Good morning. My name is Mrs. Davis. I was wondering if this is the place to ask about the summer sports camp?

Philipp   It is, Madam. My name's Philipp and I can answer any questions you might have.

Mrs. Davis   I have a twelve-year-old boy called Dominic and he always gets bored in the summer holidays. I need to keep him busy.

Philipp   We have a group for eleven to thirteen year olds, so that should be fine.

Mrs. Davis   Will Dominic be alright playing with boys a year older than him?

Philipp   Oh yes. We find that at that age group the students haven't usually outgrown each other, so they can play sport together without any problems.

Mrs. Davis   So, who does the coaching of the sports?

Philipp   We are a very professional outfit. The management are all ex-sports professionals and our instructors are usually sports science students.

Mrs. Davis   Are the students on their own with the children?

Philipp   No. They're always supervised by more experienced <u>coaches</u> **(Q1)**. Everyone receives an enhanced police check for working with children and we run our own training at the start of the summer. All our staff are ready and trained for groups of children.

Mrs. Davis   What if there are any injuries?

Philipp   All our instructors and coaches are qualified in <u>first aid</u> **(Q2)**. There is also the hospital just round the corner if there's a bad injury. It's good to have that nearby, but we haven't had to go there yet.

Mrs. Davis   I know it's unlikely, but it's always possible with that many children running around playing sport.

Page 179

Philipp   I quite agree.

Mrs. Davis   Now, I want to ask about clothing. I suppose I should make sure Dominic has warm clothing when he goes.

Philipp   Well, Dominic will be there all day and the weather can be changeable. I'd advise you to make sure that Dominic has warm clothing and changes of clothing.

Mrs. Davis   Where will the children go if it rains? Is everything outside?

Philipp   Our location is next to Wentmount School and we can use their sports complex (Q3) when it rains. It's a big place and as soon as there's any bad weather, we'll be inside.

Mrs. Davis   That's good to know. Now, what parts of the day will Dominic be at the sports camp?

Philipp   We have morning sessions, afternoon sessions or Dominic can stay all day. What would you prefer?

Mrs. Davis   I think all day. He can make lots of new friends and tire himself out. What about lunch?

Philipp   You can send him with a packed lunch or he can join in with the lunches we provide.

Mrs. Davis   What sort of food do you serve?

Philipp   There will be a basic starter such as soup or salad, a solid and hot main course and fruit (Q4) for desert.

Mrs. Davis   That sounds nice and healthy.

Philipp   Oh yes. It's a sports camp and we feel that healthy food is all part of that.

Mrs. Davis   So, Dominic will only need clothing with him.

Philipp   Well, some sports need special equipment. For example, goalkeepers use gloves and all players use shin pads. I expect Dominic will want to use his own.

Mrs. Davis   Yes, that's true.

Philipp   By the way, as Dominic's a young boy, it would be good for him to have some snacks (Q5) with him for the mornings and afternoons.

Mrs. Davis   OK. I'll make a note of that. By the way, I don't know the timings of the day. At what time does it all start and end?

Philipp   We start at nine thirty a.m. We don't do it any earlier, as the children are on holiday and it's nice for them to stay in bed a little longer than their normal school days.

Mrs. Davis   That's a good idea. At Dominic's age, children will stay in bed until midday if they get the chance.

Philipp   I've a son that age as well, so I know what you're talking about. The end of the morning session is at twelve thirty and then we start again at one thirty. The afternoon session runs to four thirty (Q6). We ask that all children are picked up by five o'clock, as the instructors will need to get home as well.

Before the conversation continues, you have some time to look at questions seven to ten.

(20 second gap)

Now listen carefully and answer questions seven to ten.

Philipp   Now, I need to know some things about Dominic. What games does Dominic like playing?

Mrs. Davis   He likes all sports. He's quite good at cricket and swimming, but <u>his preferred sport is football</u> **(Q7)**.

Philipp   OK. We do plenty of all those.

Mrs. Davis   Where do you swim?

Philipp   Wentmount School has both indoor and outdoor pools. We do lots of swimming, both for training and just for fun. It's a great way for the children to get fit and to have a good time. Now, does Dominic have any allergies or anything else we should know about?

Mrs. Davis   He's not allergic to anything. He has strong legs and he can run for ages. He was in hospital sick in December for appendicitis, but that has all cleared up now. <u>One thing is that in the winter, we went skiing and Dominic broke his arm. It's all healed now, but I think that you should be aware of that</u> **(Q8)**.

Philipp   Thank you. I've made a note of that. Now, we need to know how Dominic will go home every evening. We have a duty of care to all the children who will be with us and we need to know whether we have to look after them until someone comes or whether they will be going home by themselves.

Mrs. Davis   <u>The first week, I'll pick him up</u> **(Q9)** and then after that he can take the bus home. I expect by then he'll have lots of friends to travel with.

Philipp   Good. That will be in Dominic's notes. You can change your plans of course. Just make sure you let us know, so we can make sure he's safe at the end of each day.

Mrs. Davis   I will.

Philipp   Now, the last thing is for you to fill out an application form. You can see the information about all the fees at the end there. Pay the fees by bank transfer and put the reference number in the appropriate box on the application form.

Mrs. Davis   What happens if the course is filled up by the time you get the form?

Philipp   Don't worry about that. I've reserved Dominic a place. Just call me on the phone number on the form if you change your mind, so I can enrol someone else. <u>I'll keep the place for you for two weeks</u> **(Q10)**.

Mrs. Davis   Can I give the form in by hand to you tomorrow? I'll be shopping near here then.

Philipp   That'll be fine. Just make sure the payment is done, as the reservation isn't secure until we receive that. Once we have the form, you'll get an email within a week to confirm everything.

That is the end of part one. You will now have half a minute to check your answers.

Page 181

(30 second gap)

Now turn to part two.

Part two. You will hear a radio programme with a policeman giving a talk on crime prevention. First you have some time to look at questions eleven to fifteen.

(20 second gap)

Now listen carefully to the information talk and answer questions eleven to fifteen.

Presenter   Hello again, everyone. Welcome back to Radio Coastal. Following the amount of crime we've experienced in the local area recently, we've asked Police Constable Cameron Dawson to join us today and give us some advice on crime prevention. Good morning, Cameron.

Cameron   Good morning, Tracy. Thanks for having me here today. I'd like to give you some advice today on various crime possibilities that you might have the misfortune to experience. To start with, one common theft that the police has to deal with is that of bicycles. Bicycles can be some of the easiest vehicles for thieves and vandals to target and they are easy to sell on to others, making them a relatively attractive source of money. There are various things you can do to safeguard your bicycle, such as locking it securely and doing this in a place where thieves will find it difficult to steal. Another thing that you can do is to take a clear colour picture of your bike and make a written record of its description, including any unique features. Then you can send this to the police, who can get it back to you if it's found **(Q11)**.

Another problem in today's society is robbery on the street. While the likelihood of this happening is small, you should be aware of what you can do to keep yourself and your property safe. First of all, if you have to walk alone at night, take extra care. Stay on roads that are well lit and relatively busy. It's important not to carry any important documents, credit cards or excess cash with you and if you think you're being followed, cross the road or go into a shop, tell them your fears **(Q12)** and stay there until you're sure you're safe. Don't be afraid of knocking at someone's door in the street either and telling them your worries. Even if they don't let you in, thieves will be discouraged and probably leave the area.

Next I'd like to talk about cars. If you have a car, your vehicle will always be a target for thieves. It can take as little as ten seconds for a thief to steal something from your car, but the good thing is that most vehicle crime is preventable. Make sure you remove everything from your vehicle and don't store anything in the back. A good way to safeguard your car is to develop a regular procedure, so that you take your keys out of the car, close the windows and remove all belongings from it. **(Q13)** Follow your procedure and your car will be as safe as it can be.

We've had a rise in the number of cases of identity fraud recently. Thieves may do this in order to buy things in your name and leave you and your bank with the bill and it can be very distressing and difficult to put right. Most cases of identity fraud can be avoided through some simple common sense precautions. First of all, if you've had your bank cards stolen or compromised, make sure you contact your bank immediately to change everything. Sometimes thieves won't take away your wallet, but they'll make a note of the details. This will encourage you not to cancel the cards, but the thieves can buy things online with all the important details in their possession. **(Q14)** Another way thieves get hold of your details is when you throw away sensitive material, such as bank statements or receipts. These papers often include information useful to thieves. Stop this by shredding all the papers you think might be sensitive before you throw them away. **(Q15)**

Page 182

You now have some time to look at questions sixteen to twenty.

(20 second gap)

Now listen to the rest of the information talk and answer questions sixteen to twenty.

Cameron   I'd now like to talk a little about cell phone theft, as this has been a problem for a few years now. Having your phone stolen is a hassle. It's not just the handset you lose, it's the numbers, messages and photos too. Cellphone thieves thrive on <u>opportunity</u> **(Q16)**, so don't make it easy for them.

Here are some simple things to consider to protect your cell phone from thieves and they're all to do with being aware of your surroundings. First, take care in busy <u>locations</u> **(Q17)**, which are popular places for pickpockets, especially if a cell phone is visible in an open bag, or hanging out of a back pocket. Next, think about when you use your cell phone. Outside subway stations can be popular venues for snatch theft, as people instinctively get their cell phones out to check for a <u>signal</u> **(Q18)**. Finally, don't leave your cell phone unattended in public places. You wouldn't leave your wallet unattended, but a surprising number of people leave their cell phone on the table while they go to order a drink, or go to the rest room.

Most cell phones have a range of security features that are intended to stop anyone else accessing and using them should they be stolen. One good one is creating a straightforward PIN code that locks your handset. Another PIN feature is that you can set your cell phone to need a separate password or account ID to prevent thieves from simply resetting your cell phone to its factory setting, and therefore resetting any codes or other security features you have set. Finally, many cell phones can be traced, wiped or locked remotely, using another Internet device. These features are useful but will only protect your cell phone if you switch them on. Check the <u>user manual</u> **(Q19)** and find out how to do everything.

Knowing how to identify your cell phone if it's stolen is important for getting it back. Each handset manufactured for use has a unique International Mobile Equipment Identity number hardwired into it during the manufacturing process. Knowing this number will help the police identify your cell phone should it be stolen, as they'll need to know more than the <u>brand</u> **(Q20)** and colour of your handset. Check the International Mobile Equipment Identity number of your cell phone by checking with its manufacturer's guidelines, which should be available on their website.

That is the end of part two. You will now have half a minute to check your answers.

(30 second gap)

Now turn to part three.

Part three. You will hear two students giving a university presentation to their teacher. First you have some time to look at questions twenty-one to twenty-five.

(20 second gap)

Now listen carefully and answer questions twenty-one to twenty-five.

Professor Black   Good morning. Are we all here? Good. In today's seminar, we're going to hear a presentation from two students. The schedule says it's Lisa and Patrick. Are you both ready?

Lisa   Yes, Professor Black. We're ready. Shall we begin?

Professor Black	Yes please, Lisa.
Lisa	Well, Patrick and I are going to talk about the flower industry in Kenya.
Professor Black	The flower industry in Kenya? I didn't even know they had one there.

Patrick   Oh yes. Kenya's horticultural sector currently ranks as one of the economy's fastest growing industries, the third largest foreign exchange earner after tourism **(Q21)** and tea.

Lisa   The industry has been growing every year. The industry rose thirty-one per cent over the last five years with total exports reaching one hundred and thirty thousand tonnes per annum.

Professor Black   How did the industry begin there? It doesn't sound like a traditional Kenyan industry.

Patrick   No. The history of the export of fresh horticultural produce from Kenya dates back to the period before independence when Kenya, then a British colony, was required to help out with the running of the budget **(Q22)** for East Africa.

Lisa   After independence the industry continued to thrive with exports starting to go to Europe and thus opening up the potential for Kenya in the export market.

Professor Black   Is Kenya's climate particularly suitable for growing flowers?

Patrick   Yes. Although Kenya is on the equator, considerable differences in altitude allow a great variety of climatic conditions from the hot coastal plain up to the cool highlands. A temperate climate prevails above one thousand five hundred metres, where daytime temperatures are from twenty-two to thirty degrees Celsius and night-time from six to twelve degrees Celsius.

Lisa   Rain days are restricted to sixty to eighty days, so there's excellent radiation most of the year, which is ideal for the year-round growing of quality flowers without the necessity of green house conditions.

Patrick   Kenya has enjoyed economic advantages as well. Kenyan companies have long benefited from favourable exchange rates **(Q23)**, making their costs in Kenyan shillings and US dollars relatively low.

Lisa   The Kenyans have also set up an excellent logistics infrastructure. Nairobi, the capital city, is a major hub and is very well served by major airlines and charter operators, giving easy airfreight access to European markets and from there to the rest of the world.

Patrick   And labour and energy costs are low compared to other countries. A further advantage for Kenya is that the industry still pays no import duty **(Q24)** when sending its flowers to Europe.

Professor Black   How has the industry affected the ordinary people in Kenya?

Lisa   Pretty well. In the agricultural sector, floriculture in Kenya is the second largest foreign exchange earner after tea bringing in more than two hundred and fifty million US dollars per annum. Of course this doesn't all go to the man on the street, but it creates a lot of taxes **(Q25)** that contribute to Kenya's public economy.

Patrick   The industry does employ a lot of ordinary people though, with fifty to seventy thousand people directly employed and more than one and half million indirectly employed.

You now have some time to look at questions twenty-six to thirty.

(20 second gap)

Now listen to the rest of the discussion and answer questions twenty-six to thirty.

Professor Black   It seems like an ideal situation for Kenya with no problematic areas.

Lisa   It's not perfect and some years haven't been easy. For example, there have been problems with workforce disputes, which have not yet been wholly resolved.

Patrick   Some years as well have had problems, as high oil prices negatively affected transportation **(Q26)** fees. There have also been years when, in spite of the excellent climate, there were heavy rains or extended drought, which negatively affected the size of the crop at those times.

Professor Black   What about competition?

Lisa   Most competition comes from countries that, like Kenya, lie on or near the equator. The four leading global competitors in terms of export value are the Netherlands, Colombia, Ecuador and Ethiopia. These countries compete with each other on the same markets in Europe, Russia, and North America, and competition is getting more tense every year.

Professor Black   What's causing the increase in competition?

Patrick   It's partly due to stagnating demand, but it's also a result of the growing number of large-flowered roses and the generally improving quality **(Q27)** of the other countries' products.

Professor Black   Hasn't there been some criticism of the sustainability of the industry?

Lisa   Yes. Although things have improved, wages are significantly below a living wage, leaving workers and their families with limited or no disposable income. Finally, trade union membership is often discouraged and undermined.

Patrick   One of the biggest ongoing criticisms is about water usage. The water footprint of one rose flower is estimated to be seven to thirteen litres. The total virtual water export related to the removal of cut flowers from the area where the flowers have been grown has been colossal. The water leaves the country and the continent and it's not easily replaced.

Lisa   This has caused an observed decline in the levels of local lakes and a deterioration of the lakes' biodiversity. **(Q28)**

Patrick   There is also a problem with pollution in the large lakes that supply water for the industry. Initially, everyone blamed the large producers, but it seems that although the commercial farms around the lake have contributed to the decline in the lake level through water abstractions, both the commercial farms and the small holder farms in the upper catchment are responsible for the lake pollution due to nutrient load.

Professor Black   How can this be addressed?

Lisa   There have been calls for sustainable management of the basin through charging water **(Q29)** at its full cost and other regulatory measures, but any change in prices has been resisted and there are a variety of political and tribal barriers to getting legislation passed and enforced.

Professor Black   Are there any other downsides to the Kenyan flower industry?

Lisa   Yes. There have been some criticisms of outdated farm methods. However, more farms are increasingly looking into organic methods of pest control **(Q30)** and those farms that have implemented water-recycling and waste disposal systems have found that they are able to decrease overall costs in the long run.

That is the end of part three. You will now have half a minute to check your answers.

(30 second gap)

Now turn to part four.

Part four. You will hear a lecture on cotton. First you have some time to look at questions thirty-one to forty.

(50 second gap)

Now listen carefully and answer questions thirty-one to forty.

Hello everyone. Today in this agriculture lecture, we're going to look at the background of one of our most important clothing materials in the United States and that is cotton.

No one knows exactly how old cotton is. Scientists searching caves in Mexico found bits of cotton and pieces of cotton cloth that proved to be at least seven thousand years old. They also found that the cotton itself was much like that grown in America today. The Cotton Belt spans the southern half of the Unites States, from Virginia to California. Cotton is grown in seventeen states and is a major crop in fourteen.

The cotton growing process begins with planting. Planting is accomplished with six, eight, ten or twelve-row precision planters that place the seed at uniform depths and intervals **(Q31)**. Young cotton seedlings emerge from the soil within a week or two after planting, depending on the temperature and moisture conditions.

The growing process can be threatened in different ways. Cotton grows slowly in the spring and can be shaded out easily by weeds. If weeds begin to overpower the seedling cotton, drastic reductions in yield can result. Producers employ close cultivation and planters place the cottonseed deep into moist soil **(Q32)**, leaving weed seeds in high and dry soil. Herbicides control weeds between the rows.

The cotton plant has evolved with numerous damaging insects, and these insects, if left unattended, would virtually eliminate the harvestable crop in most cotton-producing areas. Plants infested with the leaf-feeding insects are able to counteract somewhat by growing increased numbers of leaves **(Q33)**. Many cotton-feeding insects, however, feed on the cotton itself. This reduces the yield and leads to delays in crop development, often into the frost or rainy season. Plant protection chemicals are often used to prevent devastating crop losses by insects. All plant protection methods used on plants in the US are thoroughly evaluated by the Environmental Protection Agency to assure food safety and protection to humans, animals and to the environment. Some plants are also improved by modern biotechnology, which causes the plants to be resistant to certain damaging worms.

The cotton plant's root system is very efficient at seeking moisture and nutrients from the soil. From an economic standpoint, cotton's water use efficiency allows cotton to generate more revenue **(Q34)** per gallon of water than any other major field crop. Most of the US cotton acreage is grown only on rain moisture, but a trend towards supplemental irrigation to carry a field through drought has increased in acreage and helped stabilise yields.

Harvesting is one of the final steps in the production of cotton crops. The crop must be harvested before weather can damage or completely ruin its quality and reduce yield. Cotton is harvested by machine **(Q35)** in the US, beginning in July in south Texas and in October in more northern areas of the cotton-growing area. Stripper harvesters, used chiefly in Texas and Oklahoma, have rollers or mechanical brushes that remove the whole cotton bud from the plant. In the rest of the cotton producing areas, spindle pickers are used. These cotton pickers pull the cotton from the open buds using revolving barbed spindles that entwine the fiber and release it after it has been separated.

From the field, seed cotton moves to nearby gins for separation of lint and seed. The cotton then goes through dryers to reduce moisture content and then through cleaning equipment to remove foreign matter. Cotton is then moved to a warehouse for storage until it is shipped to a textile mill for use.

Cotton is ready for sale after the quality parameters for each bale have been established. Growers usually sell their cotton to a local buyer or merchant after it has been ginned and baled, but if they decide against immediate sale, they can store. Since it is a non-perishable crop, cotton stored in a government-approved warehouse provides a secure basis for a monetary loan **(Q36)**.

An often-overlooked component of the crop is the vast amount of cottonseed that is produced along with the fiber. Cotton is actually two crops, fibre and seed. Annual cottonseed production is about six point five billion tons. This seed is crushed, producing a high-grade salad oil and a rich protein **(Q37)** feed for livestock.

One key aspect of this growing process is the management of pests. The most common way of treating pests is by aerial disbursement of pesticides. A crop dusting plane flies low over the crops and sprays the cotton with the pesticides that are in a holding tank **(Q38)** under each wing. A careful spraying schedule and pattern should be created and the cotton farmer must therefore have very careful notes on sowing and growing information. The pesticides are squirted straight down from the spray nozzles on the plane. The angle is important. If the spray is sent forwards in the direction of the plane's flight, the droplets will become too fine and be carried away in the wind or in the slipstream **(Q39)** of the plane. Some of the pesticides of course will hit the right crop, but some will be untouched. This creates further problems as the farmer will not know which areas are treated and which are not. Re-treating may result in too much pesticide on an already treated area, but not re-treating may affect crop yields. If the spray is sent backwards from the spray nozzles with regards to the direction of the plane's flight, the droplets will be too coarse **(Q40)**, which will also create uneven results. A straight down release creates the optimum medium-fine droplet spray.

That is the end of part four. You will now have half a minute to check your answers.

(30 second gap)

That is the end of listening test fourteen.

LISTENING TEST 15 TRANSCRIPT

This recording is copyright by Robert Nicholson and Simone Braverman, all rights reserved.

IELTS listening practice tests. Test fifteen. In the IELTS test you hear some recordings and you have to answer questions on them. You have time to read the instructions and questions and check your work. All recordings are played only once. The test is in four parts. Now turn to part one.

Part one. You will hear a conversation between a man and a woman as the woman interviews the man for a job.

First you have some time to look at questions one to six.

(20 second gap)

Now we begin. You should answer the questions as you listen, as the recording is not played twice. Listen carefully to the conversation and answer questions one to six.

Mrs. Allen	Good afternoon. You're Adam, aren't you?
Adam	That's right.
Mrs. Allen	I'm Mrs. Allen. Now, you're here for the cleaner interview here at the hospital.
Adam	Yes.
Mrs. Allen	Well, let's get started. I need some personal details from you first.
Adam	OK.
Mrs. Allen	Now, your first name is Adam. What's your surname?
Adam	It's Marshall.
Mrs. Allen	Could you spell that?
Adam	It's M - A - R - S - H - A - L - L. **(Q1)**
Mrs. Allen	Thank you. And what is your address?
Adam	It's eighty-two Ackland Road, Gorley.
Mrs. Allen	And the postcode for that address?
Adam	It's OG eight, six RE.
Mrs. Allen	Thank you. Next I need your mobile phone number.
Adam	It's oh seven five four three, eight four two, five nine two. **(Q2)**
Mrs. Allen	Good. Thanks. What's next? Ah yes. Do you know your national insurance number?
Adam	I do. It's MA six seven, nine five, three six F.

Page 188

Mrs. Allen	And how old are you?
Adam	I'm <u>twenty-one</u>. **(Q3)**
Mrs. Allen	Good. Thank you. Now, you know that this interview is for a part-time job?
Adam	Oh yes. I'm a student at the university, so I wouldn't be able to hold down a full-time job anyway.
Mrs. Allen	So, what kind of hours will you be available?

Adam   My lectures start in the morning at ten, so I'll be available from around six in the morning until nine and then in the afternoons and evenings, starting at around three p.m. I guess I'd want to be free by ten in the evenings. I'd be available <u>mornings</u> **(Q4)** at weekends.

Mrs. Allen   Well, we should be able to find you work in those hours. Being a hospital, everything has to be very clean and we need people at all hours of the day and evening.

Adam	That will suit me very well.
Mrs. Allen	By the way, have you had any experience as a cleaner before?

Adam   A little. When I was at school, I did a weekend job at a <u>local restaurant</u>. **(Q5)** I did the washing up and helped out with the cleaning. I had to mop down the floors and clean all the surfaces. From time to time, we had to push back all the appliances and cupboards and clean behind everything.

Mrs. Allen	That sounds like good preparation for us. Did you enjoy the work?
Adam	Yes. I liked the people I worked with, so time passed quickly and I made some new friends.
Mrs. Allen	Can we contact them?
Adam	Of course. I asked them when I left if that was alright and the manager gave me his email address.
Mrs. Allen	Do you have that with you?
Adam	Yes. It's david at apple dot com. He said he'd give a <u>reference</u> **(Q6)** to anyone who asked.
Mrs. Allen	Good. That will be very helpful.

Before the conversation continues, you have some time to look at questions seven to ten.

(20 second gap)

Now listen carefully and answer questions seven to ten.

Mrs. Allen	Well, Adam. I think we can offer you the job.
Adam	Thanks very much. I look forward to starting.
Mrs. Allen	Now, I'd like to tell you a little about what we expect in the job. You can ask questions at any time.
Adam	OK.

Mrs. Allen   So, to begin with, when you arrive, you need to check in at the staff reception, **(Q7)** so your arrival time can be logged in. This will mean that you get paid the right amount. Then, when you finish, you need to log out at the same place.

Adam   OK. I remember that. What is my rate of pay by the way?

Mrs. Allen   You get nine pounds an hour. Is that OK?

Adam   Yes, that's fine.

Mrs. Allen   Now, after you've logged in, you need to go the staff changing rooms. We provide you with green overalls to wear while you're at work, and there is a locker where you can keep your own clothes and valuables safe while you're working. You also need to wear a special hat, **(Q8)** which will prevent any hair falling out where it shouldn't. This is especially important if you have to go into the kitchen areas.

Adam   Yes, I had to do that at my last job.

Mrs. Allen   Now, if you work longer than three hours, you're entitled to take a twenty-minute break. During this break, you can do what you want. Some people go and have a cigarette or get some fresh air. We ask you not to go into the public areas during your breaks. There is a staff canteen **(Q9)** where you can get free tea, coffee or soft drinks. If you work longer than four hours, then you're entitled to have a meal as well.

Adam   Good. That will save me from some cooking!

Mrs. Allen   Now, we'd like you to start next weekend at nine a.m. Would that be alright?

Adam   Yes, that's fine.

Mrs. Allen   Before you start on that day, it's important that you come for an hour for some training. **(Q10)** We need to show you all the equipment and where you'll be working. This will allow you to get on with things straight away when you arrive on Saturday. You'll be paid for this hour of training at your usual rate.

Adam   When shall I come in?

Mrs. Allen   How about Thursday at four p.m.?

Adam   That'll be fine. I'll be here.

Mrs. Allen   Well, that's everything for now. Thanks very much for coming in, Adam. I look forward to you working with us.

Adam   Thank you very much, Mrs. Allen. I look forward to it as well.

That is the end of part one. You will now have half a minute to check your answers.

(30 second gap)

Now turn to part two.

Part two. You will hear a radio programme with a woman giving some people information about a town exhibition. First you have some time to look at questions eleven to sixteen.

(20 second gap)

Now listen carefully to the information talk and answer questions eleven to sixteen.

Presenter   Welcome back to Radio Gem. Now we're going to talk to Mrs. Stephanie French, who is going to tell us a little about the town exhibition that starts next week. Welcome, Steph.

Stephanie   Thank you very much. It's great to be here.

Presenter   So, tell us about the town exhibition, Steph.

Stephanie   Well, as you know, the town has an exhibition every summer. As usual, it will take place in the town <u>park **(Q11)**</u> and it'll last from Tuesday the ninth of July until Sunday the fourteenth of July. The exhibition serves several different functions. Firstly, it is a business exhibition, where all local businesses can set up stations, so that people can come and ask them in person about anything related to the businesses. This might range from just general interest to possible business partners setting up new deals. Given our location, the farms in the area have plenty of apple orchards, so there is one particular section on apple juice and other related products.

Another function of the exhibition is to be more like a town fair. There are always games, competitions and amusements to see and take part in. A lot of these things go on throughout the day, but also many of the amusement rides and other things aimed at children open from <u>three **(Q12)**</u> p.m. Every evening at ten p.m., the exhibition will end with a big fireworks display, which lasts for twenty minutes. This is always a popular event and the best place to view the fireworks is next to the central lake. Please note that if people plan to take their <u>dogs **(Q13)**</u> with them for the evening, be aware the fireworks often distress them. It's often better to just leave them at home rather than giving them stress.

If you're planning on spending time at the exhibition, especially if you're with children, you ought to know that there will be a variety of food on offer. There will be ranges of Italian, Chinese, Turkish, Thai food stations, along with plenty of other international options, and there will also be an open fire barbecue, with meats and <u>vegetables **(Q14)**</u> freshly grilled. Naturally, there will be plenty of drinks available as well.

If you're bringing children, make sure that they are suitably dressed. If it's hot, it can be very tiring, especially for young children. Also don't forget to bring plenty of sun screen and a hat to protect their skin. If the weather's bad, don't forget raincoats, umbrellas and think about wearing <u>rubber boots **(Q15)**</u>, as the grass areas can get very muddy if there's rain around.

Every day, there are lottery tickets sold and the winning numbers are called out every evening, just before the fireworks. Try your luck and see what you might win. Tickets are only four for a dollar, so you won't need to break the bank. If you can't stay until the evening to hear the results, just write your name and <u>telephone number **(Q16)**</u> on the back of the ticket that you leave with the lottery people and they'll call you if you're lucky enough to win.

You now have some time to look at questions seventeen to twenty.

(20 second gap)

Now listen to the rest of the radio programme and answer questions seventeen to twenty.

Stephanie   We've had a number of emails asking for information regarding where things will be found at the exhibition, so I'll talk a little about that next.

As you come in the main entrance on East Avenue, there will be the pavilion with all products to do with apples on your right. This will be an enormous marquee, holding the stations of many of our local businesses. One great advantage of this place is that it's all covered up and a good place to shelter if there's bad weather. They have their own little food and drink section as well, so you can get a hot drink or warm soup if it's cold.

On the left as you enter the exhibition, opposite the Apple Pavilion, as we call it, you'll find the section devoted to all other local businesses. **(Q17)** This too is in a big marquee and is an interesting place to wander around and see what is done in our local area. Next to this is the first aid station **(Q18)**, which can help you with any minor health problem you have while at the exhibition. They always have three people on duty at any one time and these fully trained first aiders can deal with more serious issues if needed as well as a headache from too much sun.

If you continue down the path away from the entrance, you'll find lots of stalls on both sides with various things to buy. These can include local jams and dried herbs, farm produce, such as eggs and honey, handicrafts in wood and metal, and lots of second hand stalls, where you might be able to pick up a bargain.

These various stalls go right up to the central lake. As you reach the lake, directly opposite will be the area where you'll find all the food stations **(Q19)**. There's plenty of outdoor seating with long tables and there are large areas that are covered in case you need to escape the rain or too much sun. The open tables are a great place to watch the fireworks later with an evening drink. It's a popular place, so get there early if you want to find a good spot.

On both sides of the lake, opposite each other, you'll find all the amusement rides and games that can be played **(Q20)**. These are areas of great fun both for adults and for children. Make sure that you visit these places at least once with your friends and family. It will be an experience you won't forget!

That is the end of part two. You will now have half a minute to check your answers.

(30 second gap)

Now turn to part three.

Part three. You will hear two students giving a university presentation to their teacher. First you have some time to look at questions twenty-one to twenty-five.

(20 second gap)

Now listen carefully and answer questions twenty-one to twenty-five.

Dr. Williams   Good morning everyone. Today, we're listening to a presentation by Toby and Fran. Are you both ready?

Toby   Yes, we are, Dr. Williams. Shall we start?

Dr. Williams   Yes please. You go ahead, and as usual I'll come in with various questions as they occur to me.

Fran   OK. So, we're talking about the benefits of electricity as a fuel for vehicles. To begin with, I'd like to talk about energy security here in the United States. <u>Two years ago, the United States brought in from abroad about thirty-three per cent of the petroleum it consumed</u> **(Q21)**, and transportation was responsible for nearly seventy-five per cent of total US petroleum consumption. With much of the world's petroleum reserves located in politically volatile countries, the United States is vulnerable to price spikes and supply disruptions.

Dr. Williams   But isn't US electricity generated by imported oil as well?

Toby   No. Almost all US electricity is produced from domestic coal, nuclear energy, natural gas, and renewable resources. Using hybrid and plug-in electric vehicles instead of conventional vehicles can help reduce US reliance on imported petroleum and increase energy security.

Dr. Williams   Do all electric cars get their power from outside sources or can they generate it themselves?

Fran   <u>They can if they have an onboard generator, but running one will always be more expensive than getting power from the electricity grid</u> **(Q22)**. No one would do it unless they have a hybrid car that has an onboard generator and they couldn't find an electricity charging source.

Dr. Williams   And do electric cars actually use less fuel?

Fran   Oh yes. Electric vehicles typically use less fuel than similar conventional vehicles, because they employ electric-drive technologies to boost efficiency.

Toby   <u>So, electric cars definitely have lower fuel costs compared to similar conventional vehicles, on the whole due to the low cost of electricity relative to conventional fuel</u> **(Q23)**. The fuel economy of electric cars is also highly dependent on the load carried and the slow duty cycle.

Dr. Williams   Isn't that true for conventional cars as well?

Toby   Yes, although not so much.

Dr. Williams   What other benefits do electric cars have?

Fran   One very topical benefit is of course that they can have significant emissions benefits over conventional vehicles. Wholly electric cars have zero tailpipe emissions, and hybrids produce no tailpipe emissions when in all-electric mode.

Toby   <u>The life cycle emissions of electric cars depend on the sources of electricity used to charge it, which vary by region of the US</u> **(Q24)**. In geographic areas that use relatively low-polluting energy sources for electricity production, electric cars typically have a life cycle emissions advantage over similar conventional vehicles running on gasoline or diesel. In regions that depend heavily on conventional fossil fuels for electricity generation, electric cars may not demonstrate a strong life cycle emissions benefit.

Dr. Williams   I've heard that the use of biodiesel in cars is as good in terms of tailpipe emissions as electric cars. Is that true?

Fran   Not really, but there are similar advantages. The fuel B100 reduces tailpipe emissions by more than seventy-five per cent when compared with petroleum diesel, but they're still more than the zero emissions by electric cars. <u>Using B100 biodiesel does reduce greenhouse gas emissions though, because, although the carbon dioxide released from biodiesel combustion is about the same as the fossil fuel engine, it is offset by the carbon dioxide absorbed while growing the soybeans or other feedstock.</u> **(Q25)** Tailpipe emissions also depend on which biodiesel is used.

You now have some time to look at questions twenty-six to thirty.

(20 second gap)

Now listen to the rest of the discussion and answer questions twenty-six to thirty.

Dr. Williams   Are there any disadvantages to electric cars?

Toby   Yes. One problem is the current infrastructure availability for refuelling. Public charging stations are not as ubiquitous as gas stations, but charging equipment manufacturers, automakers, utilities, clean cities coalitions, municipalities, and government agencies are establishing a rapidly expanding network of charging infrastructure.

Fran   It's still reasonably flexible though. Since the electric grid can be available almost anywhere people park, electric cars can charge overnight at a residence, a fleet facility, at a workplace, or at public charging stations. Hybrid cars have added flexibility, because they can also refuel with a <u>fossil fuel</u> **(Q26)** when there is no electricity charging available.

Dr. Williams   And are the costs of buying an electric car comparable with buying a conventional car?

Toby   Not yet. Purchase prices can be significantly higher. However, prices are likely to decrease as <u>production volumes</u> **(Q27)** increase.

Dr. Williams   I suppose that potential buyers know that they can save more money in the long run by using an electric car.

Fran   Yes. That's an aspect that the marketers of electric cars really push hard. I suppose that's natural.

Dr. Williams   What are all the different ways in which people can save money?

Toby   Let's see. The initial costs can be offset by fuel cost savings, a federal tax credit and <u>incentives</u> **(Q28)** provided by the relevant state.

Dr. Williams   What about maintenance?

Fran   Electric cars need maintenance just as conventional cars do, but a significant difference is the battery. The advanced batteries in electric vehicles are designed for extended life, but will wear out eventually. Several manufacturers of electric vehicles are offering eight-year or a hundred thousand mile battery <u>warranty</u> **(Q29)**.

Dr. Williams   This must be a great perceived drawback to people considering buying an electric car.

Toby   Yes, short-life batteries are a significant disadvantage to electric cars and if the batteries need to be replaced, it can be a significant expense. However, battery prices are expected to decline as <u>technology **(Q30)**</u> goes forward and as increasing numbers of batteries are manufactured.

Dr. Williams   Well, that seems to be a good place for a break for you. Do any of the other students have any questions for you?

That is the end of part three. You will now have half a minute to check your answers.

(30 second gap)

Now turn to part four.

Part four. You will hear a lecture on twins and autonomous languages. First you have some time to look at questions thirty-one to forty.

(50 second gap)

Now listen carefully and answer questions thirty-one to forty.

Hello everyone and welcome to this lecture on speech development. Today, we're going to look at twins and how they are theorised to often communicate with each other in their own language.

Twins are regularly reported to invent languages of their own that are unintelligible to others. These languages are known as autonomous languages and, despite current belief, this is not a <u>rare **(Q31)**</u> phenomenon. Autonomous languages exist in about forty per cent of all twins, but often disappear soon after their appearance.

So, how does this language formulate? The theory behind a twin language is that siblings are so close to each other and rely on each other so much that they don't have as much of a need to communicate with the outside world, and so they make up their own idiosyncratic language that develops only between the two of them. These siblings actually do not necessarily have to be twins. The typical situation is one in which two or more close siblings grow up closely together during the language acquisition period. If an <u>adult model language **(Q32)**</u> is frequently absent, the children use each other as a model and acquire language imperfectly. If a model is completely absent, the children copy other sources, maybe the television or radio, and probably do not create a recognisable language.

In all known cases, any language actually created by close siblings is made up of onomatopoeic expressions, various <u>invented words **(Q33)**</u> and words from the adult language adapted to the constrained phonological range of young children. An autonomous language will lack coherent morphology and the word order will be based on pragmatic principles. Because of all this and because the words themselves are hardly recognisable, the language may turn out to be completely unintelligible to speakers of the model language.

A lot of research has gone into autonomous languages. Neither the structure of these autonomous languages nor their emergence can be explained by other than <u>situational factors</u> **(Q34)**. Research studies seem to indicate that what appears to be a twin language might actually be two children with the same delay in phonology, which is how children put speech sounds together into words. The delay in phonology is usually due to a lack of models to copy, which are usually parents. Children tend to establish speech sounds in the same general order and they often make identical types of <u>errors</u> **(Q35)** in their speech. Children with phonological delays have speech sound systems that don't develop as would be expected, and this makes it hard to understand their speech. Some researchers now believe that what is often described as a twin language is actually two normal children whose speech sounds are not developing as would be expected.

Researchers further theorise that these speech sound errors can be <u>prolonged</u> **(Q36)** in twins or close siblings, because each child has a partner who seems to understand him and uses the same type of speech as he does. While this does make their speech a kind of a twin language, as the two children seem to understand each other when others cannot, it's also a delay in sound development that probably needs to be addressed by <u>speech therapy</u> **(Q37)**. Not surprisingly, studies have also linked the presence of an autonomous language to language delays in later school age years.

Parents of twins or close siblings who have their own language should not have to panic! There seems to be a small percentage of children who have both their secret language and who are able to communicate effectively with their parents in real language. These children will switch back and forth between their own language and their developing mother tongue, depending on who they're talking to. It's also important to note that researchers have found that not all children who have their own language will go on to have language delays. An autonomous language seems to be only a <u>risk factor</u> **(Q38)** that children will struggle with speech and language. However, it will indicate that an evaluation by a speech-language therapist might be beneficial in helping to decide what's really going on.

So, what can a parent do to help their children develop normal speech? Firstly, parents are the most important guide to language acquisition and enrichment. What parents say and how they say it will directly impact their children's development of speech sounds and <u>sentence</u> **(Q39)** duration. Therefore, parents should talk to their children as often as possible, describing what they're doing and why they're doing it, what's around them and what's happening. Secondly, it's never too early to start reading to children. Research has indicated that even infants can benefit from this. As all children grow, <u>reading</u> **(Q40)** should be a daily part of their routine and it will improve their language, vocabulary, attention and future success. Twins will benefit from this even more.

So, what eventually happens to the autonomous language between twins or close siblings? In most cases, the private language begins to disappear spontaneously, after a low-key intervention, or when the children enter school, interact with other children, and immerse themselves in the more powerful lingua franca. The children might shift to the use of their secret language every once in a while and this is just normal. However, if they are given the right training, they will not develop delay in language learning.

That is the end of part four. You will now have half a minute to check your answers.

(30 second gap)

That is the end of listening test fifteen.

Made in the USA
Las Vegas, NV
05 April 2023

70165182R00109